FROM SERPENT TO SAVIOR

A Memoir

Bill Mitchell

FROM SERPENT TO SAVIOR.

ISBN 978-1-66785-552-3

DEDICATION

To my brother Dave,

whose courage to confront me about my

addiction, was, I believe, the seed sprouting

my awareness, subsequent recovery

and a new path in life.

PREFACE

This book is intended as a truthful memoir, omitting names and circumstances where it would hurt or harm another person; it is for reference only with experience, hope, love and strength, as well as a caring attitude of all those in denial, suffering and recovery. It is intended to aid people in their struggles with alcoholism, drug addiction, any addiction and to inspire a thought-provoking recovery, one day at a time/one person at a time. It is not intended as medical or self-help advice, nor is it a religious book. It is meant as an expression of the power of faith to heal and aid in recovery. This memoir is referenced for search purposes only in the categories of alcoholism, addiction, drug addiction, recovery, self-help and transitions. The information herein is to help you identify with alcoholism and even drug addiction (or both), and to inspire healing and a successful life through self-examination, with support or support groups, as well as professional help. It is not a substitute for consulting with a counselor, doctor, physician, psychiatrist, psychologist or therapist.

Acknowledgments

Meg, my incredible wife, soulmate and companion in life for her love and patience over the last 33 years. 8 children, 14 grandchildren and 3 great grandchildren for all the joy and incredible love they have given.

My brother Dave for his example, love and especially his courage to question my addiction that led to my recovery and MaryAnn for her contagious faith and example.

Nephew and niece, cousins and all my relatives for their lives contributing to whom I've become.

The One Bread One Body members, too many to list, for their love and faithfulness in meeting each Friday for 25 years, sharing the Word of God, and for their courage and determination in saying "Yes" to reaching out to the needy of the world.

Close friends Lawrence, Guy, David, Sal, Mark, Billy, Ginger, Terry, Marcel, Kathy, Theresa, Jack, Pat, Fr. Michael, Fr. Joe, Fr. Charlie, Fr. Caverly, Fr. Steve, Fr. Tommy, Fr. Scott, Sr. Christa, Frank, Kathy, Jimmy, Kathleen, Mary, Don, Dan and all those too numerous to mention that have impacted my life throughout the years.

Special thanks to Dr. Bob Webb for his devoted time

and editing expertise, and his wife Diane for her added input in finishing this book.

To granddaughters Rachel and Madison and Jordan for their formatting assistance; and; Elaine and Karen and Marsha for their editing assistance; and especially to daughter Shawn for her book review.

Lastly, to my wonderful parents Bill and Mary Mitchell whose unconditional love and shrewd Irish advice, passed down to my brother Dave and me, helped us define and shape our lives.

TABLE OF CONTENTS

PART THREE

PART FOUR

PART FIVE

PART SIX

Introduction

Whether you are a teen experimenting for the first time with alcohol, a college student pledging a fraternity/ sorority, making new friends, beginning your career, networking or entertaining potential business partners, alcohol or even drugs are often the center point of most social activities, even more so today with the explosion of social networks. You may feel something is not right— work, home, financial or even personal problems, and that the only way to deal with them is an indulgence in drugs or alcohol. There may come a day when you realize there are far too many "indulgences" in your life.

Are you willing to admit there are problems, or do you tell yourself, "This is the last time?" As often as you may have tried to quit, when the going gets tough, do you tell yourself, "One more won't hurt?" With just one more, our desire to quit is once again squelched.

Does a friend's call with an invitation or you need a break from what you're doing, so you arrange to meet up with friends again, or an old friend is visiting from out of town? All reasons to celebrate; all reasons for using drugs and/or alcohol? If so, are you doing yourselves a disservice with the choice of your merriment? We are constantly deluged with temptation. Temptation is too great to resist, and the immediate thought is a "yes" response to the drug of choice, often knowing you are once again on the Road to No Return. Is there help, or are we looking in all the wrong places? Are you doing the same thing over and over and getting the same results, but wishing for something different?

This book was written by an expert on self-destruction, someone who has been there and back, through thick and thin, to the brink of self-destruction and near death. This is a story of a thirty-five-year recovery that began on August 2nd, 1986. The date is worth mentioning. It is an important date never to be forgotten – the day I turned my life around and changed forever.

This is the story of what led me down the road to addiction and what changed my life and brought me back to sanity. It is an awe-inspiring story that culminates in a long life of charity and spirituality; a life worth living every day. A story of healing and falling in love all over again. A story of broken relationships with family and friends, healed through peace and love, without the mind-altering poison that makes one do crazy things (self-centeredness). I share things in this book that I wish I had not done; many things I cannot change or go back and fix. I made a life -altering choice to go forward and start anew each day, one day at a time. This is the story of my desire to help others, knowing I could not give others what I myself had not received from God, and often acting through others who took the leap of strength and courage to become sober. This book shows you how to go forward, falling in love with family and friends again, falling in love with yourself again, learning to love life again, and believing in a power greater than Self, a higher power called God, a God of understanding, the supreme creator of all good.

This story of my journey to a new way of life will hopefully inspire you to make spirituality the center of your hope, instead of the bottle or any other addiction. Herein you will find a blueprint, for healing and recovery with all addictions, as prescribed by the Alcoholics Anonymous (12 Step) program along with specific spiritual exercises, placing you on a path perhaps you always dreamt of, but something kept getting in the way: you. Or perhaps you will find the courage it takes to reach out to someone to heal a broken heart. It will not always be easy, but there is One who will never leave you, and that One is God. You will know the amazing joy of following in the footsteps of your Creator; you will be energized to want to give back, to love others again by developing a spiritual relationship with your higher power, God.

The writing of this book was my lifelong desire to help others as I was helped by other recovering alcoholics, and ultimately by God—truly a wisdom given to me through continuous efforts to learn of the God of our creation. My hope in telling my story is for others to identify with me, to hear their own story in mine, and when ready, for others to tell, share, and possibly write their own stories—however long it takes. We know there are no quick fixes in life. There are highs and lows in the *Bottle of No Return*, short lived, leaving us with yet another disappointment, to pick-up the pieces over, and over again, getting the same results every time, along with the same feelings of being a failure. You are invited to read all or some of this book—your choice. I focus on both the people in my life, and the prayer life that propelled my healing toward love. This book chronicles my life from a teen to a successful man in all areas of my life, from addiction to conversion, *From Serpent to Savior*. Come; take the journey with me, as I continue to write my life story every moment of every day with the Lord by my side, living out my dreams in abundance with spirituality as my-breast plate. You can too.

PART ONE

Journey into Addiction
and the Path to
Destruction

Chapter 1

The Serpent is Hatched

MY STORY BEGINS in my hometown of New Haven, Connecticut, on Long Island Sound, located halfway between Boston and New York City. It was the summer of 1962. I was with three of my buddies in my friend Benji's red Oldsmobile convertible. I remember being in the back seat while we were driving around town on a warm Friday night, having a grand time, listening to the latest tunes of *Loco-Motion* by Grand Funk Railroad, *Monster Mash* by Bobby "Boris" Pickett, and *Peppermint Twist* by Joey Dee and the Starliters. The plan was to go into the liquor store to buy some beer and vodka, booze as we called it, and none of us being of age didn't stop us; one of my friends had a fake ID. As he entered the liquor store, the rest of us had our eyes glued on the door in nervous anticipation. Would he succeed? After what seemed like an eternity, he appeared carrying a bag full of beer and a bottle of Vodka. What a coup! *Too good to be true*, I thought as we drove off, music blaring. We were set for the night.

As an 18-year-old, youngest of my parents' two sons and grandson of Irish immigrant grandparents, this was my introduction to manhood. Dad, local sports icon in New Haven in his heyday and owner of a few saloons, was my role model growing up. In Ireland, pubs were traditionally considered refuges for males.

This began to change when immigrants came to the United States. Irish wives and mothers played a major role in reversing this trend by discouraging their sons and husbands from frequenting these establishments. The Irish were only one of many groups who shared the culture here. Personally, I was pulled in both directions. My mother's parents though Irish, were teetotalers, but my father and his father were definitely Irish drinkers.

Though he liked his shots of whiskey and a few beers here and there, sometimes more, I admired my father's heart because he was always for the underdog. While his strong faith and compassion for the lowly, didn't impact me much then, it would 25 years later, help define who I would become and my primary purpose in life. Unfortunately, his drinking habit accompanied by all his sporadic drunken escapades would follow me as well. But on balance, we were close. He was my hero. He was a gifted athlete growing up. His football and baseball prowess earned him a college scholarship as well as minor league baseball player in the Cape Cod League at Woods Hole in Falmouth, Ma. He taught me nearly all I knew athletically. He was the major reason I went on to become an all-state hockey player. I was also adept at tennis and golf, but that I learned from my mom, a six times state tennis champion.

Though my father had quite a reputation for partying and drinking in his bachelor days, my mother succeeded in keeping him in check, often warning of the ills of drinking, as she had learned from her teetotaling parents. I remember, it did not take but a few times Mom asking Dad to go for bread and milk and him returning 2-1/2 hours later, after hitting the gin mill for a few pops, for her to figure out that sending along son Billy, that being me, would eliminate Dad's stopping at the gin mill. Wily Dad, though, wasn't deterred. He still stopped at the gin mill, but now he would take me in to sip on a cola and nibble on a bag of peanuts as he knocked off a few before returning home in only an hour. All seemed to be fine when we got home so I guess an hour was better than two-and-a-half.

The evening's escapade was significant, because it

was my first attempt at getting really high and venturing into the exhilarating world of adults. After all, I had just graduated from high school. Summer break had offered me a few chances to have a beer or two here and there, but tonight was big—really big. Tonight, I, along with my three buddies, would validate our manhood by getting high. Tonight, would be my initiation into the Irish tradition of raising your drink and exclaiming, "Slainte", Gaelic for "Good luck and God be with you." I still have vivid memories of Dad from my childhood. Of Dad at frequent parties with lots of relatives, corralling my uncles off behind the refrigerator, pouring whiskey shots, and all of them raising their shot glasses high in the air shouting "Slainte." Their facial expressions of joy and jubilance said it all. Irish songs and jigs would soon follow. Now I would join them.

The evening flew by as we drove around, singing along to the radio, taking swigs of vodka and washing them down with gulps of beer, until the whole bottle of vodka was empty. It was not long before I started feeling the effects of the alcohol: a sudden rush coming over me. Things I normally wouldn't do in a sober state like singing out loud, cursing, and telling dirty jokes became part of my new elation. This new feeling was all and more than it was cracked up to be, I thought to myself. The rush became euphoric as I surmised, "I have arrived; I am a man." My ecstasy was almost too good to be true.

Finally, in the wee hours of the morning, my friends dropped me off in front of my house. Everything during the evening had been a total blast, up to the point when I got out of the car. Everything went rapidly downhill from there. Staggering helplessly, I fell to my knees, numb, semi-conscious, blind drunk—in a state of total oblivion. After a violent regurgitation, I lay on the driveway sickened with a complete feeling of betrayal and disillusionment. My anticipation of drinking had been that I would experience the fun and enjoyment that I saw others having, and that I had felt earlier in the evening. The after-effects of pain and sickness were not the climax and total ecstasy I expected. This booze, which I now see as a serpent, had sucked me into this drunken state and in the end, spewed me out to suffer. It was like a close friend's betrayal that caused me to become totally disoriented and disenchanted. My father came and somehow got me into bed.

My feeling on the first morning-after was typical: horrible hangover, feeling bad from head to toe, but as the day wore on, it became more manageable, and amazingly, as the light of day grew near to the dark of night again, I was physically able to again entertain the idea of going out and taking another drink. The weird dichotomy of it all was in the ensuing pattern of anticipatory ecstasy and the knowledge of the probable ending, the hell of inevitable sickness. It all seemed worth it. The thoughts of getting high immediately trumped the thoughts of the awful consequences later on.

The lessons my parents relentlessly tried to instill in me to learn to say, "No," was obviously not effective, because the calls from friends the next evening found me with a titillating desire to re-experience the newfound high that I discovered the night before. Despite the pounding memory of my adventurous conclusion, I was ready, and, even eager to say, "Yes, I am willing and able." The initial stage of a form of insanity was, without my knowing it, settling in. The pattern of drinking, hangover, and starting over again the next day was creeping into my being, and it continued night after night that summer.

It was not long before booze had become part of my life like a newfound friend. It became one of my life's necessities, like the air I breathed, the water I drank, and the food I ate. New discoveries about the serum called booze and what it could do amazed me. If I was depressed, it could catapult me into a false oblivion of joy; if I was consumed with fear, it would unshackle the chains; and if I was lonely, it immediately surrounded me with friends with whom I desired to be locked up in fantasy. It wasn't long before booze became the priority in my life, and I found myself searching for those friends for whom booze was the center and focus of their existence too.

During that same summer break, while waiting for my first semester of college to begin, I was working as a laborer for my father, a stonemason. The work was great but the starting time each day at 6:00 a.m. was horrific, especially after entertaining the bottle the night before and the ensuing hangover headache. The serpent, now in its infancy stage, began taking on another element—placing me and others in danger without considering their safety or mine. Drinking while driving did not matter. The thought of an accident, injuring or killing me, or killing others, failed to enter my mind, and my concern was completely turned off. Carelessness and recklessness started to become a big part of my behavior.

One morning on the construction job, after a whopper of a hangover, I was told to make some cement in the cement mixer. I began shoveling sand, pouring water and emptying large bags of cement into the large rotating mixer. It wasn't a difficult job, but because I was so sick from the hangover, it was easy to let my guard down, and I ignored the possible danger. I continued shoveling sand into the mixer—almost in a stupor from the night before, and then suddenly, the head of the shovel caught in the rotating mixer blades. The handle of the shovel instantly lashed back at me knocking me unconscious.

Bloodied, with a huge knot on my noggin, I was somehow able to shake off the cobwebs and, despite my father's protestations to take the day off, stayed on the job. Little did my father know at the time that this accident, that could have caused severe injury or death, was a result of alcohol abuse from the night before. In my own mind I must have labeled the incident as resulting from inattention, rather than as a result of too much drinking the night before, because my drinking went on unabated. This was my first close call with death as a result of booze, but not my last, but predictably, I did not make the connection. I survived, summer break was gone all too soon, and the scene changed to a university campus.

The summer after high school seemed too short, especially with my newfound friend, the bottle. However, I entered Quinnipiac University with great anticipation and expectation. This stage of life was set for a degree in accounting, following the footsteps of my Uncles Joe and Jamie, both CPAs. I started off on the right track, but with campus life and the demands of keeping up with the fast pace of studying and homework, academic life soon became very stressful, even though I had a pretty clear picture of how hard the work would be. The focused path I had thought to follow soon became lost among poor choices of partying instead of studying. I fell behind in all my classes.

Cramming for exams, as well as last-minute work that should have been done days and weeks before, produced grades that were barely passing. In retrospect, the situation was producing a mindset that was the beginning of delusional decision-making. I could be confronted with choices such as studying for the next day's exam or going to a party. I knew that studying for the exam was the correct choice, but a voice in my mind told me, "Don't worry, you can do both." In my mind I heard, "I am Smart! I can fit both in! Party some! Then come back and hit the books!" This thinking quickly became a seemingly sensible consistent way of deciding what I would do, but this newfound philosophy put me on the road to disaster.

"Birds of a feather flock together" is what my mother would always say, and boy, she was spot on. It wasn't long before I ended up associating with other students that knew where all the fraternity and sorority parties were. It was not long into my collegiate life that I began juggling library study time and party time. Each week would have at least a couple of parties going on, and I did not want to miss any of them.

Unfortunately, I teamed up with another student, who was a close friend of mine from the days of growing up. Studying with him was not helpful, because he had the same problem I had: "A budding alcoholic future." He had just flunked out of the state university and was now attending the local university with me. However, he had become adept in limiting partying just enough to get the "proper" grade—or so it seemed.

He also introduced me to the world of fake identifications. A fake ID was magic! It was our ticket to obtain the booze we needed. My mind began to work on the problem of getting one for myself. Amounts of alcohol consumption went up too. The thought of having just one beer became an absurd notion. Drink until I get a buzz was my new rationale. Capital GIQ's (Giant Imperial Quarts) became the beer of choice (extra-large quarts for half the price). Little did I know that "Have a quart of beer..." was the beginning of a recipe for absolute certain failure. Mixing study and alcohol soon put me in the precarious position of having to cram for the next day's exam.

From early in the semester, the drinking bouts progressed. Every week, the stints of alcoholic drinking superseded studying, which led to me blowing off classes. This became an increasingly regular practice. Of course, it also meant taking the exams unprepared and thus rolling the dice in hopes that I could guess an answer correctly and get a passing grade. Failing test scores then prompted me to drop the classes that seemed hopeless to try to pass, and I completed the few remaining courses with barely passing grades. Unfortunately, this became yet another pattern in my life, a bad habit that continued to get worse.

The weeks passed quickly, and the first semester ended with me on probation following my finals. This was not a good start for a freshman in college. Rationalizing the problem as not enough focused studying, my solution was to slow down on the drinking and partying. This was easier said than done! Obvious now, but not then. Accelerating highs from getting boozed up were too much fun. Justifying to my parents why I was put on probation after one semester needed a whole new concocted story. Deception was beginning to sound authentic, so merely by saying to them that the courses I took were really difficult, I thought I still had a grip on things. Next semester should see much better results.

Christmas break passed fleetingly! It became a two-week drunken spree, and, as if I didn't have enough on my plate, it was on this spree that I elevated my habit to drinking in bars. Though I was 18, and the drinking age was 21, this did not matter, because I now had my own fake ID. My brother Dave, four years my senior, served in the Navy and luckily left his ID at home one evening during Christmas break. It was a small matter to change one digit under "date of birth" and Presto! It seemed too good to be true—only 18 and now able to drink in bars and nightclubs, albeit illegally. The serpent was alive and well.

Spring semester of 1963 began with great intentions to study, study and study harder. In doing so, I thought things would work out. The problem with this solution was my having not addressed the growing drinking problem, especially now that I could drink anywhere with a fake ID. Soon I recognized the same pattern of bouts with the bottle, partying with the buddies, not studying, and failing classes began to repeat just as before despite my mind's glimpses of hope. In my thinking, I believed my same actions would have different results without giving up the alcohol. I later learned this was called "Stinking Thinking." I blew through the semester as a total disaster, academically barely passing, and barely avoiding probation, but the merriment all seemed well worth it at the time. Years later, I would think, "I wish I knew then what I know now."

Chapter 2

Summer Break — the Serpent Grows

DURING MY FIRST failing collegiate year at Quinnipiac, I did a lot of "Stinking thinking"—doing the same thing over and over, thinking things would be different. I am not sure whether Benjamin Franklin or Albert Einstein was the first to state, "The definition of insanity is doing the same thing over and over and expecting different results." How well this fit me at that time! I am sure the serpent was pleased.

I had not taken on outside work during my freshman year, so that I would have more time for study, but instead it gave me more time for partying, boozing it up, and failing my classes. Looking back, all I had accomplished were near failing grades, being on probation, and feeling tremendously dejected after my first year of college. It was just too embarrassing for me to return to the same academic surrounds after two disastrous failed semesters. I was aware I looked stupid. However, I did not give up hope and decided to try new surroundings. I enrolled in a new local college, New Haven U., but decided to take a semester off before diving in again.

During summer break in mid '63, having left Quinnipiac, I found abundant and well-paid work in the construction business. With money to spend, my choice was to party with alcohol. The more I made, the more I spent, including often buying drinks for my under aged colleagues, and encouraging their delinquent habits. I was breaking the law by helping minors, but this was not my concern. With time on my hands and money to spend, the stage was set for a further descent into the serpent's pit. I began to associate with some really bad people.

Wacky Woods, in particular, 6' 4" and 240 pounds, was nothing to mess with. Regarded as the meanest and toughest guy in town, he was well known by the police authorities. If you looked into his eyes when he was sober, you immediately sensed a wildness and unpredictability about him that cautioned you not to agitate him in any way. If you looked into his eyes when he was high on drugs or booze, you sensed a death warning. In short, Crazy Wacky Woods would be best left alone or else—

instead we became friends.

One night while drinking at the local bar called Midnight Tavern, I lamented to Crazy Wacky Woods about my girlfriend sadly breaking up with me because of the sudden irresponsible change in my behavior. She was a college girl now, and the writing was on the wall that I was going in the wrong direction. Her mother also knew of my recent drinking escapades and forbid her to see me ever again. I was becoming a different person, and with the high of alcohol, I sometimes became aggressive and belligerent.

Well, Wacky Woods had heard enough and decided to intercede on my behalf right then and there. We drove over to my girlfriend's house to talk to her and parked a few blocks away from her parent's house. My dilemma was how to get hold of her, since I was forbidden to see her or call her. Wacky Woods had the solution. Her bedroom was on the second floor, and before I knew it, Woods had scaled the outside of the house to the top of the roof on his way to her window. He soon had me up there with him. I had called out her name as loudly as possible without giving away our whereabouts. When there was no answer, he started tapping on the window to no avail. He then escalated his tapping, calling out her name louder and louder.

Suddenly, without warning police squad cars were racing towards the house, sirens wailing. Off the roof we jumped, running to escape. The police spotted us and after a hot pursuit they cornered us. We were too drunk to feel any pain and were smiling ear-to-ear while they handcuffed us. My new buddy kept coaching me repeatedly, "Don't say anything. Just plead the fifth." As we were placed into the back seat of two separate squad cars, I turned to see Wacky in the other car laughing hysterically. All I could think was how terrified I felt and how disappointed my parents would be, and he was laughing! This was my first arrest, and not exactly what I had envisioned after graduating from high school and entering college.

During the wait time at the police station, I began feeling as if addiction, maybe, was slowly settling in me; I thought I recognized developing patterns of alcoholism. My drinking escapades definitely were wrong patterns! Then there was Crazy Wacky Woods smiling, yelling again to me, "Don't tell them anything Mitch," a nickname he called me. "Just plead the fifth." I asked myself, "How could one year of bad decisions take me from over-achiever to feelings of being a total failure?" My bad decisions had taken me from my dreams of college and career to finding myself flunking out of college and sitting handcuffed-in a police station. I was an average Joe from a good family on the right side of the tracks, good upbringing, and a good neighborhood. "So how did things go so horribly wrong? I kept on asking myself. But all that came to me was an old Irish ditty: "Tell me who your company is and I'll tell you who you are." There I was in the middle of the night, pleading the Fifth Amendment at the encouragement of Crazy Wacky Woods during our police interrogation.

The police knew my famous mother who had won state tennis championship's six years in a row, as well as my legendary father who played professional minor-league baseball and football. Both were well-known, upright citizens in the community, and devout Christians. How disappointed my parents were in me! The picture of my father walking into the police station is one of the worst memories of my life. As Dad approached me, I could see both the disbelief and disappointment, not to mention the fury in his eyes. Through my parents, I was released, but my friend Wacky Woods' previous arrest record did not help him any, and he was booked and sent to jail.

I have come to see that the insane way my life was going was the serpent's venom of *booze* piercing my body and blood stream. In spite of it all, I didn't learn my lesson from this arrest. Over the next few weeks, my skirmish and brush with the police did not serve as any warning that my drinking was in fact endangering my life and hurting the people I loved the most.

It wasn't long before it was made clear again that I hadn't learned anything from my past escapades. I was sitting in O'Malley's Tavern again near closing time with my friend Danny, and he said he had had enough and was leaving. I declined Danny's ride home and chose to have a few more drinks. Within minutes, two guys walked into the bar, and I could sense that these were "really bad characters." As they sat down in the bar stools next to me, introducing themselves as Mad Mac and Big Jim Borelli, the bar lights started blinking for last call. It was almost my last call.

Mad Mac offered me a lift home. I accepted and we walked out to the car, but things soon began going wrong. The route they drove was not toward home but in the opposite direction. After driving several miles, the surroundings became deserted and wooded and the car slowed down. When it stopped, Big Jim pulled me out of the car and threw me to my knees. Mad Mac began screaming at me, accusing me of hitting on his wife at McNeil's Bar a few nights before. He then pulled out a gun and put it to my head. Continuing in his shrill tone, he yelled, "Start praying Romeo, nobody messes with my wife." Nervously, I shouted, "There is no truth to it." He became even more incensed and delusional. I again pleaded with him, telling him that I had nothing to do with his wife. Big Jim Borelli, sensing that things were getting out of hand, stepped in and started to beat me up. They threw me back into the car, drove for a short while, and dumped me off at a highway embankment.

Somehow, I got back to the road and limped back to my friend Danny's house where I could clean myself up before heading to my parents. My life seemed to be totally out of control. This was now the second close shave with death due to my drinking. Boozing was becoming more than an isolated incident.

A few weeks later, at Midnight Tavern, I ran into Crazy Wacky Woods again, newly sprung from jail, and he told me that he was going down to a night club in New Haven. Would I join him? Of course, so we drove the distance and entered the night club that was packed with people. Suddenly a bunch of thugs burst in and dragged Crazy Wacky Woods out of the bar. Intoxicated, I thought I could help, but luckily some friends quickly informed me that these thugs were not to be messed with, and they restrained me.

It developed that the guys that took Wacky Woods outside were part of the local mob and connected to a mafia family. Apparently, the mob came to get Crazy Wacky Woods, because the night before-in a drunken stupor, he had gone to Sam Stefanato's house looking for his girlfriend, who happened to be the mob boss's daughter. While at the house, Wacky Woods apparently was asked to leave, but instead started yelling, and screaming and knocking down the mob boss's white picket fence. In his stupor, Wacky Woods kept yelling expletives until he eventually left, leaving property damages behind him. So, the mobsters had come to the night club to teach Wacky Woods a lesson. After dragging him out of the night club, they pummeled him to near death. When the ambulance arrived, he lay unconscious on the ground, his face flowing with blood and covered with opened cuts everywhere.

Once I got home that evening, I again ruminated on recent events. Here I was, an average kid who had chosen the path to alcoholic addiction, with an arrest and two near brushes with death from gang-fighting, having a gun put to my head and pummeled by hoodlums for allegedly flirting with someone's wife, and now narrowly avoiding a second beating trying mistakenly to defend a friend, all as a result of my drinking. Again, on summer-break, trouble seemed to follow me everywhere I went, but while all this was happening, usually in a drunken state, it never occurred to me that maybe the booze was the root of the whole problem.

By mid-summer, a new phenomenon would appear in my life, 'blackouts' from my drinking, which, I was told, is a "cognitive, psychological and behavioral impairment of specific neurotransmitter receptors of the brain, causing a temporary amnesia state." With these 'blackouts', I began to wonder how could *booze* destroy all my life goals, cause untold angst and grief with my parents and thrust me into the doldrums of doom and gloom? All in one year with association of drugs, derelicts and undesirables of society, who still protected me during bouts of alcohol as the youngest of the group! Easy!

If only I had listened to my mother's wisdom, the series of simple and bad decisions would not have led me astray. There was no thinking before acting, only impulsive decisions based on my desires. If only I had learned to say "No" to delinquent friends and my own recklessness. Who needs friends that say they care, and then are willing to entice you with your addictive behaviors while watching you fail? My father warned me several times to "Watch who you surround yourself with. When the chips are down, your so-called friends will sell you short." In the end, these friends enabling my addiction dragged me down and sold me short, while I sold my own soul. All the friends had the commonality of drinking problems of their own, spiraling out of control, and in retrospect, each of them had initial stages of alcoholism to varying degrees. I went from one bad relationship to another. The serpent had us all, but summer was not through with me yet.

One morning I woke startled by the voice and face of my father nudging me, "Wake up! Wake up!" My dad had found me sleeping outside of our house in mom's Rose Garden, clutching a bottle of gin in one arm and a mailbox I had stolen from the night club Tara, where I had apparently been drinking the night before, in the other. This must have been a bazaar picture for my dad to see; he queried me as to what happened, and how I had gotten into this predicament. I had no answer for him; I had no recollection. This was Blackout Number One of the many yet to come.

On another occasion after a night on the town getting completely blasted, I had no recollection as to where I had parked my car. The last thing I remember that night was desperately looking for my car before I passed out. The next morning, a tapping on the car window woke me. Evidently, I had gone to sleep in the backseat of someone else's car parked in their driveway. I do not know who was more surprised, me or the man at the window. He was screaming at me to get out of his vehicle. My head felt ready to explode, and I scurried off. Realizing my dilemma, I stumbled to a phone booth (still around in the early '60s) and summoned a friend to come fetch me, and help me look for my car. I had no recollection as to where I parked it.

It is safe to say that my drinking problem had settled into an addiction. The serpent in my case, clearly known as alcoholic drinking, had a firm grasp of me. I kept reviewing how far I had fallen. From being an all-state athlete and a high school graduate to flunking my freshman year in college. One-and-a-half years of close encounters with death, and bad choices of companions, (unquestionably drunken guys like myself): had rendered my life out of control.

Chapter 3

Serpent Full Grown
More College — Jail — Klan

ALTHOUGH I MANAGED to save my life from skirmishes with the law and a few brushes with death, I did save enough money to give this new university a try. I found an apartment and a former fellow student to be my roommate. He and I played hockey together in high school, and initially I believed this was a good match for both of us. Unbeknownst to me, my new roommate, Skip Muldoon was even more of a drunk than I. As one might guess, the weeks before the fall semester of 1963 at New Haven U were not without incident.

Our apartment was a just a few blocks from Yale

University, where there was never a shortage of parties and plenty of bars. It was an understatement to call this a poor choice. One evening, my roommate and I arranged to meet some friends at O'Leary's for Friday night happy hour. Dressed in an islander floral designed shirt, probably looking 14 years old instead of my age of 19, with the legal drinking age still 21 years old, I stood at the bar waiting to be served, knowing it was illegal to serve alcohol to any under-aged persons at any establishment. My accompanying friends knew the bartender, so I was served without question. Feeling smug, I made a trip to the men's room (the John as we called it) and the smugness quickly disappeared. I was approached by two men, who identified themselves as with the vice squad, and who immediately asked for my ID card. In my brain fog, I figured I was toast and blurted out honestly that my ID was modified. They confirmed that indeed it was a fake, and I was taken to the police station for booking.

My mind raced, *Here we go again!* My second university and I were off to a dreadful start even before it began. However, that evening, my father eventually bailed me out of jail. Again, I was released due to Dad's reputation with the police as a familiar athlete in the area, a former baseball and football star.

Though the incident shook me up a bit, a few weeks passed without a major incident and I somehow unbelievably completed fall semester orientation at

New Haven University. With renewed determination I had a vision of possibly overcoming my drinking and partying problem. Although my apartment was situated in the midst of a college party-town, I began classes determined to succeed. I chose my courses confidently, so as to succeed in my studies and with new dedication to working hard, and not falling behind in my course work.

The fledgling, first time, hockey program began practice and try-outs. Knowing I had been a high school all-state hockey player brought Coach to my door. He also knew I had not met my grade-point average previously, but now with excelling grades, I met the requirements to follow my initial dream to play collegiate hockey. Miraculously, I did finish both the fall and spring semesters with passing grades, and had aced at least one of my courses, and that provided me academic motivation. Life was progressing!

After one year at New Haven U., I again spent summer break working as a laborer in the construction business, again making copious money. There were the usual weekly parties with wine, women and gambling, but I managed to stay out of serious trouble. Drinking was still a problem but I began to think I could handle it.

My fall registration began with careful selection of my favorite classes. Then came the icing on the cake. As the fall semester opened, Coach summoned me that the hockey season was to begin. The team assembled within weeks, and to my surprise, included many players with backgrounds similar to mine. The team consisted of rough and tough guys, most dropouts from other colleges, and all were first class caliber players. One of the team members Big Buddy Albrick was another former all-state player. Unfortunately, he too was a major alcoholic. He was shortly suspended at mid-semester for being arrested for the sale of narcotics. A few years later he was found dead, riddled with bullets, an apparent drug deal gone bad. Another example of a good kid getting wrapped up with the wrong company, arguably as a result of his budding addictions.

That could have been me, but things had turned around. My focus and hard work had paid off with a new beginning. Life was terrific! I balanced my academic studies well with traveling for hockey matches and I was proud of my accomplishments. My new motivation kept me out of trouble and was thrilled playing collegiate hockey.

Fall semester of my second year (my second semester of playing collegiate hockey) continued smoothly, again with surpassing grades and astonishingly A's in a couple of my courses. My grades were in check for fear of flunking and not playing collegiate hockey; not to play hockey would have been unbearable.

Unfortunately, though, my improved new behavior and lifestyle would be short lived. A series of events would derail me again, and my poor, erratic, unthinkable decision-making would see the serpent pulling me once again down the slippery slope of academic failure. Partying and drinking appeared again as the unbelievable insanity of alcoholism began to consume me once more. My dream of living responsibly day-to-day, to be successful in academia and play hockey evaporated into thin air. In retrospect it seems perhaps that whenever life becomes routine, the serpent takes over. By the end of that semester, my drinking had turned into major binges. The stage was set for the next dramatic event, and it appeared right on schedule.

One night, sitting on a barstool during the Christmas break, an Air Force recruiting sergeant next to me, spent the next couple of hours selling me on a career in the armed forces. The sergeant expounded that the military would help me find responsibility by serving our country. He went on to explain that boot camp would shape me up, give me direction in life, and help me receive what is most needed in life to succeed, accountability. He further explained that by enlisting, all my college education would be paid in full by Uncle Sam. It seemed like a great recipe for a new lease on life! "If you like it, you could make a career of it with a pension in twenty years."

In my drunken stupor, retirement with a pension and government benefits for life while still in my early forties sounded pretty awesome and immeasurable. Enlistment sounded completely awesome in wiping away all the mistakes I had made over the past few years and in taking away my sense of failure.

Although inebriated, I felt alive for the first time in a long time, with a sense of calm, a feeling of redemption. I had a sense of certainty about enlisting, in part, because my older brother Dave was serving in the United States Navy. A new dream was emerging. Nothing could get in the way of my new life opportunity, the potential success in military service. Wow! I was ready. The good sergeant finally confirmed our meeting for the next morning and then said good night. With a couple more beers to celebrate, I sat marveling at the new possibilities that lay ahead of me, but in the next hour, things would change dramatically.

No sooner had the sergeant left than a drinking buddy showed up whom I had not seen in a long while. As I sat proudly and enthusiastically telling my friend what had just happened to me, he responded to it with total disdain. He called my decision to enlist pure lunacy the sergeant's sales pitch big hype. "Do you really think that's all true?" "We're in the middle of the Vietnam War, and you will probably be shipped straight to Nam."

As I sat listening to him in an alcoholic haze, he continued, "Come with us. We are leaving for the warm sandy beaches of South Florida in the morning." A mutual friend was a student at Miami University, and my buddy went on to exclaim, "We could be there in two days…fun, sun, party city. Do you want to come?" It was the serpent in disguise!

My decision in the next few minutes would influence the rest of my life. Thinking to myself, "Surely, I wouldn't decide to dismiss the idea of enlisting?" "That would be the height of lunacy and hypocrisy." Plus, even if I decided not to enter military service, my college life was at an all-time high with average grades, and I was still playing college hockey. Guess again. The thought of sunny Florida and partying with my friends during the 'cabin fever' of a Northeast winter, almost immediately fueled my impulsivity and trumped the decision I had made just two hours before to enlist. Within minutes, I was talked into going with my friends to South Florida instead of enlisting in the military. My mother's advice— "You have to learn to say 'No' to your friends"—never had a chance.

Before I knew it, we were off on our 1,200-mile trek for the fun, sun and beaches. I negligently and recklessly abandoned any thoughts of rationally considering the adverse consequences of such an irresponsible decision. Thoughts of completing my education and the possible career in the military instantaneously vanished with the delight of wine, women and song—a vision of sun and sand. Even though the first to attend college in the family, albeit my father was awarded full scholarship to Vermont

U., but during the Great Depression, short lived after two semesters, with his father beckoning him home to help support the family.

The thought of disappointing my parents did not occur to me. The insanity of my addiction to the wiles of the serpent once again lured me, sucked me in to the abyss of my youth. The image of four young men from the same flock of undeniably budding alcoholics, fleeing the winter blues to a lifestyle of booze, drugs, gambling and women, took precedence over my future.

We made the whole journey without incident until the Florida-Georgia border, where we received a justly deserved speeding ticket. As the South Georgia trooper was writing us up, he drawled, "Y'all have two choices—appear in court tomorrow or pay the fine right now." That was called kangaroo court. We chose the latter and drove to the Police Station and settled up. By now evening was setting in and while on our way out of town, driving on a dark rural road heading back toward the main highway, we suddenly spotted a big white and red glow in the woods ahead of us. As we drew closer, we were stunned to witness a burning cross with a crowd of people around it. Our driver slammed on the brakes as he yelled out the window, "Shit head KKK."

Within seconds a few trucks sped from the burning cross area in hot pursuit. Thankfully, one of us had the good sense knowing we had a northern license plate and could be mistaken for 'Segregation Freedom Fighters', and we instantly sped off. Thank goodness we did. Luckily, we made it to the main interstate without incident and were on our way again to south Florida.

My two week's turned into three months stay in Florida would not turn out to be a disappointment, as it was all I envisioned and more. No sooner had we arrived than we were out on the town for a night of major drinking and dancing. Then we flopped at a fraternity house in Miami as guests of our friend. Upon awakening the next morning, our fraternity friends announced that a gorgeous girl in a convertible was outside waiting to pick me up. As I tried to clear the cobwebs out of my brain and focus on making sense of this improbability, I had no recollection of this person in an inopportune blackout, and in addition knew absolutely no one in South Florida. My friends, of course, encouraged me to see who was in the convertible, so, although completely befuddled, I quickly freshened up and made my appearance. I was convinced that I had never seen this girl before in my life, but, stunned by her beauty, I approached her.

She explained how we had met the night before at the local Murph the Surf's Ale House, had danced the night away together, and had made plans to go to Key West in the morning. I was confused and exhilarated at the same time. How did she know so much about me but I didn't even know her name? On our way to Key West, she made a quick stop at the Doral CC where she worked. While she ran in to retrieve something, I quickly opened her glove box to see her registration. Finally, I knew her name! Sherry! That first date driving down to the Keys turned into almost daily meetings for the next two or three months, and even with money becoming scarce, our friendship developed into a serious relationship.

However, my lack of confidence caused me to fear that I could not keep up my commitment to the relationship. Between my lack of money and my irresponsibility, I impulsively retreated by flying back to the comfort and security of my family's home in New England. The habit of abruptly withdrawing from people, causing them disappointment, became a pattern I adopted so that "Fight or Flight" regrettably became a part of my youthful character, especially with alcohol in me most of the time.

Back in Connecticut, my obvious immaturity, insecurity and lack of direction in my life haunted me, but kept me turning to the bottle for enlightenment and encouragement. My life was changing dramatically again for the worse; I was drifting backward and starting again to hang with undesirable men.

Chapter 4

Serpent in Control
Marriage — Multiple Failures

A FEW WEEKS later, while at home resting, I was summoned to the phone. The caller was a friend, Franny Finn, whom I hadn't seen in years—we had played high school hockey together. By the tone of his voice, he sounded amused and excited. Then he laid the bombshell on me! "I am sitting here at the beachside night club (Connecticut) with two girls that are trying to find you. They somehow out of the crowd asked me if I knew of a guy by the name of Bill Mitchell and I responded that I was indeed a friend and that I would ring you up."

It was none other than my girlfriend Sherry from

South Florida with Joyce, her sidekick... Somehow without knowing my address, they showed up in my hometown. Without knowing a soul, she miraculously met someone at a night club who knew me. The phone call from her left me absolutely stunned. With no other choice, I drove down to the nightclub, picked them up and brought them home to my parents where they stayed a few days until they were able to find a place for themselves.

We picked up where we had left off, dating nightly for the next several weeks, and, you guessed it, I partied hardy. To make a long story shorter, she settled in, got a job and our relationship blossomed again. But, true to form I was not bothering to consider future consequences and some weeks later, in the second bombshell, she broke the most startling news, "I am pregnant!" Faced with the first real "yes" or "no" decision in my life, abortion could have been an option, but would not even be considered, because both of us held firm moral positions on this issue. Fear crept into me! Taking care of a wife and child seemed daunting. We talked it over and concluded, "How could I support both of them when I couldn't even take care of myself?"

Finally, we decided the confidence in our love for each other seemed sufficient to warrant saying "yes." However, the fun and excitement of our night life, and the serpent of my thriving addiction had not gone away. Ultimately, whether or not our reason to marry was valid, we made a decision to do so.

Now, first and foremost, was the difficult task of breaking the news to my parents. Fortunately, both were supportive. Next step was driving the 1,000 miles to Michigan to meet her parents and to ask her father for his blessing. Meeting her parents in Michigan went well, but after a few days there, I discovered a challenge. Both of my future-in-laws were teetotalers. Wow! They were teetotalers in relationship with a budding alcoholic. I say, "budding" because, of course, I was not thinking clearly on the point and the serpent was well established.

Within a few months back in Connecticut, we were married. We spent our first wedding night in a neighboring town, I drank myself into oblivion, and blacked out again. Faced with my second major life changing decision, it did not take long to decide to move away from the familiarity and security of my hometown, a thousand miles west to where her parents lived in Michigan. Soon we were packing our meager belongings into our 1962 Pontiac Lemans convertible and driving to Michigan. The next several days of our honeymoon revolved around my getting high on alcohol. By the time we made it to our destination, I had sobered up for my teetotaler in-laws. My new challenge was staying sober while living with my abstinent in-laws.

When we arrived in Michigan, my father-in-law told me he had a connection with a new General Motors plant opening locally, where he secured an accounting position for me. Perfect beginning to my new career, since accounting and finance was what I majored in while in college. Although our move to the Midwest was clearly traumatic, it soon turned to our advantage; good fortune started coming our way. All those seemingly wasted semesters in college proved to be fruitful after all.

Everything seemed to be turning up roses as things went well for us at first. Within the first year, we gave birth to a beautiful baby girl. Things continued going well. Within the next six years, we had three more beautiful healthy children, plenty of money to own Cadillacs, Corvettes, a swimming pool, and country club membership just for starters all at the tender age of 27. Life was good and on the surface, it appeared we had the ideal family, health, wealth and happiness.

But something was lurking beneath the shallows of my inner desires, the booze still haunted me. The serpent was on the prowl, only I did not notice it. My drinking habit was still there and particularly tormented me in the mornings after. Hung over, I felt disgusted with myself and began self-deprecating. My wife interrogated and harassed me each time, and in return I retaliated and lashed back with verbal abuse.

Drinking out on the town, dancing and partying were weekly events, often unfortunately without my wife. When I awoke after a binge, I was even more disgusted because I could not totally recount where I had been the night before. The binges eventually turned to verbal and physical abuse on my wife. She would justifiably question me, but I was guilt ridden and did not want to hear it. I knew I could change but didn't and I did not want anyone in my face about it. Our life was like a Jekyll and Hyde marriage. From the outside, it seemed ideal, but underneath the veil was disaster in the making, and I was in complete denial. Most of the time I was thinking my drinking was my only fault. I knew I had messed up, yet I didn't think I did anything wrong. With a haughty turn, I would walk away from my wife during arguments saying, "Don't bug me."

Although we seemingly had everything any young couple would aspire to achieve, the serpent had entered my life with a firm grip and had cunningly crafted my marital demise, which I perceived as not drink related. I was simply a functional thirsty drunk and still able to perform well at work. Over the next ten years, slowly but surely my dependency intensified, causing incredibly irrational behavior of unthinkable crazes, that would ultimately devastate not only me but my beautiful family as well.

Eventually, my version of the functional drunk sordidly put my job in jeopardy with frequent tardiness due to hangovers; my drinking had gotten out of control, but I could not stop. There were far too many close calls with car crashes that became common occurrences while driving intoxicated. For example, one night while celebrating with a few coworkers, I became inebriated and on my way home in a snowstorm I missed a sharp, right-hand turn. My car, traveling at a high speed catapulted over a gully and into a corn field. Stunned and startled, but unhurt, my car now stuck in the field, I staggered the several miles home in the snowstorm.

I also was unknowingly becoming a bad influence on others. One day after work a co-worker and I hit a local gin mill for a few pops. The few pops led into way too many. We eventually left half in the bag. Unfortunately, he drove the opposite way on a dead end street, hit a tree and was killed instantly. Was I becoming a negative influence as a result of my alcoholism? Was I in a sense becoming a serpent to others?

One day a coworker, who knew my intent to resign and go full time into my rapidly growing Amway business, slipped the word to my boss that I was about to leave my job. I was soon summoned into the Comptroller's office... He and I had a personal relationship in addition to our business one. We were golfing buddies, and his wife was a client in my wife's Hair Salon.

After several attempts by him to explain the great career I had with GM, his plea to reconsider leaving the company was all for naught. Deep down inside I felt insecure in continuing my company obligations because of my increasing tardiness and calls in sick, all because of my habitual drinking habits. All my fellow coworkers were baffled as to how I could leave such a great career, but again I knew deep down that my drinking problem had become far too unmanageable. With the writing on the wall, I put my resignation in. I had no other choice.

Luckily however, I did have another option that GM was not aware of. My wife and I had also decided to venture into her family farming business. My father-in-law had no sons, and his dream was to treat me as if I were his own son, to work and grow to the larger farm that he had always desired by expanding acreage he was presently farming. To me, this was an enormous opportunity not only for me but for my family. As 1974 dawned, dreams also were setting in of having our two sons one day join in the business as well. I was stepping into a ready-made gigantic opportunity with no monetary investment. With thousands of acres, silos to store the harvest, barns to house the livestock, tractors as large as semi-trucks that could pick 8-10 rows of corn at a time, I jumped in with both feet.

My father in-law already farmed two thousand acres of corn, wheat and soybeans in addition to buying and raising approximately 2,500 hogs. The new business was fascinating, and I soon grew to love it, as I became adept at it. It also accommodated my drinking habit, especially in the winter months when my father-in-law spent the winters in Florida. However, I was learning the business, making money and since my father-in-law had only two daughters and no sons, I had a bright future as his partner as well as a secure future for my wife and four children.

After a few years, we too were able to enjoy our first winter vacation in Florida. Fate couldn't have been any better for us, with winter vacations in Florida, and a thriving business at home with unlimited potential. However, on one trip south in the spring of 1976 away from the cold Michigan winter we became totally immersed in the aura of Florida winter at 70-degree temperatures, golf everywhere, and nightclubs galore to dance and party any time. The serpent was only sleeping, impulse rose again, and we were hooked. That first vacation proved to be life-changing for all of us. My brother Dave, my only sibling, had already moved to Orlando, and encouraged us to move as well. My wife and I discussed it and convincing my wife to move was not hard since she had lived several years in South Florida, where we met.

We were swept up in the fun and sun as temperature reached 80 degrees in February, and almost without thought we decided to sell out, pack up, and move to Florida. Unbelievably within a few days, my dreams of building a farming empire were shattered; my opportunity slipped through my fingers like water. I once again traded a potentially bright future for the dreams and fantasies of fun and sun. After settling my affairs in the farming business and selling our Amway distributorship we moved and bought a house in Central Florida, and both became employed. But within a few months, I had newfound drinking friends for late night binges, and things began to unravel again. My carousing caused violent fights with my wife, and our marriage was on thin ice once again.

Most of my co-workers were heavy drinkers, single, and partiers. I soon became sucked in and joined their partying into the wee hours. My focus shifted in a circle from drinking, carousing, golfing back to more drinking, and soon added drugs to my repertoire of addictions. I was experiencing what I thought was a good life. My boss was my drinking and golfing buddy, so there was no worry of being fired. What else was there?

My marriage continued to deteriorate. On a weekend trip to Miami things went big time bad. While there, I partied hardy, got crazy high one night with drugs as well, and in a zoned-out state, I decided to come clean with all the sinful, less than faithful things I had committed in our marriage. In retrospect I realized that all the bad things I did were when I was in the state of intoxication. However, it still didn't occur to me that I had a disease called alcoholism and that the serpent of addictive alcoholism had become almost part of my DNA. I wanted to be honest and start anew; I wanted to clean the slate and ask for her forgiveness and to start a fresh beginning. That declaration would prove to be my accurate confession, and I would never again in my life be unfaithful, but it was too late; I was making things far worse rather than better. Unfortunately, my wife wasn't ready to "forgive and forget." She looked me in the eyes and told me that as soon as we returned to Orlando, she wanted my ass out, and don't ever expect to come back.

Finally, after uncounted drinking bouts, late nights out, and verbal and physical abuse, my world with my wife came to an abrupt end. By 1981 she had had enough and filed for legal separation with a divorce one year later. I was inconsolable and distraught. The realization of losing my great wife and children was finally settling in.

Chapter 5

Serpent Loose
Marriage # 2 - Disaster Looming

MY BEAUTIFUL FAMILY and all our dreams had gone up in smoke after moving to Florida. Even with the misery I inflicted on my family and myself, I had discovered and experienced my children's mercy, love and forgiveness, even with all the broken promises, missed family excursions, and late-night tirades that imposed on the children; even in spite of all the anguish and moments of disdain and disappointment my four beautiful children suffered, I am now forgiven and loved. It was a couple of years of deep heart ache before their unconditional love could readily welcome me back into their lives. This enlightenment still could not stop me from unplugging the cork in the bottle; I still chose booze over all the people I loved closest to me. In my despair, my drinking accelerated with my unharnessed life as a bachelor. It is not hard to imagine how out of control my drinking became with no accountability at all. I was totally immersed in a world of my own, having fun, playing golf many days of the week and partying hardy at night.

Life emerged again when one day I received a call from my boss, another once-in-a-life- time memorable moment. He was at the Masters Golf Tournament in Augusta, GA. Inviting me to join him, he instructed me to load the trunk up with cases of beer and drive up to the Tournament. Overly elated at the one chance to experience the Masters Golf Tournament, I wasted no time in loading the trunk and off I went, radio blasting, popping beer, smoking a cigar, thinking about all the fun that was about to happen. About an hour out of Augusta, I looked in my rearview mirror and to my horror saw flashing red lights. My worst nightmare ensued with getting pulled over by the highway patrol.

I had a big problem! Not only did I have a trunk full of beer, but a 16 oz. open can between my legs. As the State Trooper walked up to the driver's side window, I slid the beer in between the seats. When told I was speeding, I heartily apologized and told him, "I am on my way to the

Masters and anxious to get there." I apologized humbly again saying, "I will keep it down." Miraculously, the State Trooper gave me a warning, firmly repeating for me to keep it down and commenting, "Have a great time at the tournament." I finally arrived and things were set. A week of wine, woman, gambling, drugs and strolling around Augusta National CC. For an addict it doesn't get much better than this. Finally, I was back home, miraculously without incident, and life had returned to normal. Working, honing my golf game and partying at night were my priorities.

One day after I entered and won a local golf tournament, accepting the first-place medalist trophy with a score of 73, I was approached by a woman named Suzette. She invited me to join her for drinks at her table. It wasn't long before I discovered she loved golfing and loved to get high drinking. Soon thereafter, I jumped into a relationship with her, knowing I was a full-fledged drunk, living the euphoric life with a mate who enthusiastically joined me each night, matching me drink for drink, and without any objection. *I've hit the jackpot*, I thought.

On a three-hour road trip to the 1983 Ryder Cup Golf Tournament in Palm Beach, Suzette and her girlfriend Marge polished off a full bottle of Bailey's Irish Crème. I exclaimed to Mike, Marge's husband, "Boy am I impressed!" She loved the boozing and was as crazy about golf as I; she seemed like the perfect match at the time. Within three months, she suggested we get married, and one month later Suzette and I were 'hitched up' before the *Justice of the Peace*, who happened to be Marge, at the country club where we first met. As we were saying our "I Do's", I noticed my father had a look in his eyes that I will never forget. Without saying a word, his eyes were telling me, "Son, are you sure you know what you are doing?" Ignoring my father's perceived signal after the vows it was time to *let the party begin*—my new wife and I with my parents and friends celebrated the night away. Within weeks of my marriage to Suzette, to my shock and sudden surprise, we were separated. Our separation and reconciliation situation went on for a couple of years— the alcohol brought the worst out in both of us with verbal and even physical battles.

My brother once commented to me that I was going to wear my suitcases out going back and forth. Our little sprees became a drain on our purse-strings as well. Eventually, I started selling some real estate that I had accumulated during my first marriage to support our sprees and vacations. We thought these excursions would cement our relationship, but instead, our drinking got worse, and our lives and relationship became unmanageable.

About this time, another of the most important life-changing events in my life occurred. My brother Dave, surprisingly at the urging of my new wife, met with me for lunch. He proceeded to suggest that I had a major drinking problem. I was both appalled and embarrassed that he had the audacity to mention such an absurd thing to me. How intrusive, I thought, and how so far off-track was his assumption. Sure, I did get into a lot of family quarrels as a result of my drinking; sure, my jobs over the last twenty years suffered and were affected by my drinking; sure, I lost my family with children largely because of my drinking, but to say that I had an uncontrollable problem was preposterous. I had no clue that I was in total denial and was unwilling to admit it. My brother went on to recommend that I see his psychiatrist friend to assess my problem. I reluctantly agreed and under protest went, telling myself it was only to appease my older and wiser brother, but it was really for my barely-hanging-by-a-thread spouse.

After the first consultation, the psychiatrist told me point blank that I was unequivocally an alcoholic. She recommended that I attend an Alcoholics Anonymous (A.A.) meeting, emphasizing as soon as possible. She also recommended that I immediately enter a thirty-day treatment center. What absurdity! I thought to myself, "What a totally incorrect and severe assessment." Thinking that one AA meeting would not hurt, I attended with my wife, who had thankfully consented to go with me. As we entered a smoke-filled room, I quickly perused the situation, and sized up the people. A sorry bunch of drunks lost in life. These meetings are probably good for them, but it is quite clear that I do not belong here. After all, I have a good job with stature, a great-newly built home and associated with the doers and shakers at our country club. As we left the AA meeting, I promised myself I would never return, confident that all this fuss about me being out of control was utterly absurd.

After another family consultation with the psychiatrist, I consented again, under protest, to enter the hospital. Here, I experienced my first real feeling of humiliation. After spending weeks in treatment, I finally came to realize that I had a drinking problem—I became totally enthusiastic about a future in sobriety. That feeling changed somewhat when my two daughters Shawn and Mary came to visit me in the treatment center. After explaining the benefit of the treatment center and the willingness to stop drinking, my daughter Mary stunned me when she asked me a question, "Dad, does this mean that you'll never be able to have another drink for the rest of your life?" POW! Befuddled, shocked and stumped for an answer, I thought to myself, *possibly, after I'm cured,* . My response to Mary was, "I guess so."

The first hurdle in recovery was admitting I was an alcoholic and totally powerless over my addiction and totally powerless over alcohol. The second hurdle was overcoming denial and admitting my life had become totally unmanageable. Except, there was one problem! I actually believed that I could, would and was fully capable of changing my own life, affecting my own recovery, by myself. The solution seemed simple, "Just say no." I told myself that when the urge to drink overcomes me, just *pray* to my higher power. My higher power as I learned as a child growing up in the Roman Catholic Church was the Holy Trinity: Father Almighty, The Christ (our Savior Jesus) and the Holy Spirit; three persons in one. In trying to convince myself of my own willpower, my mind said, "Do not give in to the lurking adversary within, the serpent."

Totally confident that the combination of the A.A. meeting and the treatment center rehab had solved any future drinking problems, I went on my way with this illusion of grandeur. However, the lurking Serpent knew this was a grand opportunity to again lure me back into addiction. My refusal to attend AA meetings regularly, and to seek out a sponsor who would keep me accountable for my sobriety, my lack of willingness to work the 12-step program, and my denial in thinking that I could do this by myself, together would put me right back where I began, in the bottle.

Although I had learned intellectually through my weeks of treatment that the serpent of alcoholism was baffling and cunning, I continued to rationalize going it alone. I would soon learn first-hand that stinking-thinking often works in the guise of denial, although the next several months after leaving the treatment center proved uneventful and from all appearances my life showed promise of being sober and productive.

Then tragedy struck as it does for all of us. My father, ill for several months, entered the hospital with a condition growing rapidly worse. I visited him in the hospital the night before he died with my two sons Billy, 14, and Stephen, 13. Growing up in a New England Irish Catholic family, we were taught that life was tough, and you must be tough to survive and to thrive. Hugging, kissing or crying and telling one another "I love you" was verboten. "Life is great for those that don't weaken," my mother would say. For some reason that night in the hospital with my sons Billy and Stephen, I felt an inner prompting, almost compelling me to embrace my father. Without hesitation I embraced my father and for the first time told him how much I loved him. He responded in kind by telling me how much he loved me. Billy and Stephen each hugged him and expressed their love for him.

The next day I received a call at work from my mother that Dad had died peacefully. At that moment, I realized that there was no time to waste. Far too many years had already been wasted in my selfish escapades. There would be no more delay in telling those nearest to me how much I loved them before it was too late. I had a total change of heart realizing that life is short and every minute counts.

In addition to deep sorrow, losing my father brought a variety of emotions into every vein of my being. The most immediate desire that overcame me was to care for someone other than myself. My first action was to console my mother who had almost completely depended on Dad for just about everything. My mother was a sports icon in her early life, a tennis champion, basketball phenom and later a golf star. She was accustomed to having people admire her and my father had faithfully and graciously guarded her for 48 years of marriage like a proud warrior.

For a while after Dad's passing, my sobriety allowed me to rethink my life. My father had instilled in me some particularly important lessons and virtues to live by, but unfortunately during my drinking days I did not adhere to them. I did better when I quit drinking, on the road to sobriety and restoration of my sanity.

My father was a deeply devoted Catholic Christian. He had the heart and soul of our Creator and Lord Jesus. In my 41 years of life, I never knew Dad to have missed going to Sunday Mass. This was his weekly priority, and as I matured became mine as well. I recalled listening to him expound on issues of war and peace, and he always chose peace—that same peace that dwelt within him was undoubtedly the peace of Christ abiding in his heart. From that peace emanated forgiveness, mercy and love, all of which permeated his being. Little did I know at the time of his death that he would become my greatest role model for the rest of my life. Soon thereafter my mother Mary resettled near brother David and me and adapted well in carrying on with her life in the community.

The next several months passed without incident, but something unthinkable was about to derail my life.

Chapter 6

Serpent Put to Sleep – Lashes Back

WITH MY NEW life of sobriety, my marriage to Suzette was surprisingly calm, devoid of violent arguments and verbal exchanges. One morning during Christmas week, sitting at the kitchen table with her, I was struck with a shocking and preposterous thought. As she was about to pour herself a glass of wine, I grinned and blurted out, "One little drink for me to kick off the holiday?"

Suzette looked at me, surprised and probably expecting me to say, "I'm only kidding," as I sensed her underlying fear, but I hesitatingly beseeched again, "One little drink to kick off the holiday. Not two or three or more, but just one single solitary drink." The words were uttered not without an inward sense of apprehension and alarm as I recalled what I was told in treatment, "Drinking is completely forbidden in recovery." Yet, I had a dominating confidence that I could handle just one drink. Surely after all the weeks in treatment, educating myself about the disease and the hazards, I could not and would not allow myself to fall back into alcoholic binging again.

What a coup! I had sucked her into letting me have it. My weakness and the frailty of unstable recovery, had once again allowed me to succumb to the serpent and its addicting power. I would guard against falling back into the claws of addiction. In the ensuing days and weeks, I came to believe that I was in control, when I had actually conned myself and my wife. *What a coup, again!* Unfortunately, it was only days before I was off to the races drinking heavily.

I was convinced that I could control my drinking with sheer willpower, because I could keep in mind the horrific memories of my drunken past and the maddening path it had created for me. I was certain that I could drink responsibly. After a few days sitting at the bar at our club we belonged to, I convinced my wife that nursing one beer wouldn't hurt anything. To my delight she consented. Was I on my way down a slippery slope again and didn't know it? How could that be after spending weeks rehabilitating myself in the treatment center and subsequently months of sobriety? Have I forgotten the path of destruction I inflicted during my 25 alcoholic years of addiction? Was I being lured in again by the wily Serpent? After a few more days at the club, I again convinced her that nursing two beers would be acceptable and safe. Inside me the serpent lurked and smirked, telling me to lighten up and jump back in with both feet.

Then I began sneaking drinks, thinking that I was deceiving my wife, as the alcoholic patterns consumed me with a vengeance. However all would come to a screeching halt in the next five months, when she separated and our marriage was on the verge of collapse, but incredibly this was not much concern to me. Still thinking that my life was in tune and I was in charge, I thought I was fully capable of keeping my addiction manageable. I was free to drink however I pleased.

One night after my short attempt at sobriety, I was back drinking again with my golfing buddy/boss and his wife. They invited me in for a nightcap, which turned into two and three and me staying overnight. Insanity once again surfaced. At 1:30 a.m. I unthinkingly began to berate him for having the inexcusable oversight of running out of liquor. After all, I did not care that he was my old friend, or that he was my boss, or that I had to actually get up and go to work the next day. My boss woke me at 6:30 a.m. I still couldn't figure out how or why I had exhibited no impulse control over my mouth earlier. I dejectedly struggled to ready for work. Totally disgusted and enraged with myself, I filled up with self-hatred and self-pity. How could I be so foolish, so weak, and then allow this to consume me? My certainty of my plan of the day before to quit drinking was liquidly erased from my mind. How could this have happened again?

Not surprisingly, my drinking kept getting worse. Almost reluctantly, I regressed to self-destructive behavior of heavy and uncontrollable drinking. I lost all confidence in myself and my ability to stop drinking. At this point, I had no resistance to quit but would again reconcile with Suzette. Fortunately for me, I had a great paying job and an alcoholic boss that loved golf as much as I did. One morning at work with a massive hangover, I erupted verbally, arguing with one of the company's executives, chastising him with vulgarity of a drunken sailor, and threatening him with physical harm. Immediately, I was called into the General Manager's office, where my behavior was declared intolerable. I was given the choice to be demoted or leave. Not having the confidence to go out on my own, I chose the demotion with a large cut in pay. Under protest I was assigned to a space in an adjoining vacant building, where I would be more isolated from the rest of the employees. There I could try to generate business without infecting the rest of the sales force with my negative, contaminating attitude.

Poof! Just like that, an income approaching six figures was gone. In my remorseful desperation, I decided to call it quits with the bottle again, except for the stinking thinking that badgered me. Now the unenviable task of explaining the loss of income to Suzette was frightening. I was already on the outs with my disillusioned wife, whose hope of a new life was once more vanquished by yet another tyrant rage after a night of drinking escapades with my boss. We argued violently, and I proceeded to wash away my stress and painful fear of the unknown in glass after glass of straight whiskey.

The assurance and confidence that I had always found in the bottle that alleviated my crippling pain of stress and fear had disappeared; the alcohol used for the past 25 years did not dispel my stress this time around. These dreadful feelings kept haunting me no matter how much I drank, and my stress did not disappear. For the first time in my life, I began to experience the helpless feeling of losing my mind. I was not comforted by the booze and was approaching the hopelessness of insanity and powerlessness as they say in Step One of Alcoholics Anonymous. For the first time, the serpent became not my friend but my enemy. Seemingly, the serpent ignored my emergency call, and I felt God was nowhere to be found. After the realization that alcohol would not relieve my fear and stress, my feelings compounded to the point of hyperventilating, and ultimately passing out to free myself of the pain weaving through my mind.

The next morning, desperately realizing my dilemma, I again made a conscious decision to finally, once and for all, call it quits with the bottle. I would reconcile with my wife yet again. Relief and confidence engulfed me—joy permeated my entire body with the thought of quitting for good. A titillating sense of relief both calmed me and kept me on edge the next day at work and throughout the whole day. I began to dream of all the great possibilities of my future in business while in a sober state. I knew that most all of my problems in life stemmed from my alcoholic drinking, both personally and professionally. As I looked back on life, I discovered that I didn't get into trouble every time I drank, but almost every time I got into trouble was a result of my drinking. As the day ended, I couldn't wait to get home to share my dreams and optimism with my wife and begin my new life of sobriety, free from the shackles of the simpering and skulking serpent that had destroyed my first family, caused periodic separations in my second marriage, and disrupted most business opportunities.

As I drove half-way home that day, ready to quit again, a dreadful thought entered my mind like a slithering snake: "Let's stop and have that one last beer." The enticing voice continued, "It will be the very last beer of your life—kind of a celebration to begin a new life of sobriety, a new life as a responsible father, sober husband

and flourishing businessman."

I immediately dismissed the idea as dangerous and sheer-insanity, consciously moving on to another thought. But once again, my mind was bombarded with the same temptation. I recklessly swerved into the parking lot of a package liquor store, flustered that I would immediately convince myself of one last beer. With my hands on the steering wheel and my head bowed to the horn, I thought to myself, *Just one, the last drink of my life. No more after this one.*

Once inside the store, I peered into the beer case and instantly decided, "What the hell, it's my last one, might as well be a 16-ounce can." As I reached in for the one last drink, my fleeting mind gratuitously decided to drink a last binge, and instead I grabbed three 16-ounce beer cans. Before I could get out of the parking lot, I popped the first can. Ecstasy! Within 20 minutes, I had downed all three cans. Helplessly, I stopped at a bar to have one last drink, and thereafter had no recollection of the night, even the next morning.

For the next several weeks, I drank with total reckless abandonment. There was no remorse, no beating myself up, just hard drinking as often as I could manage. I was on that slippery slope of no return that leads to nowhere, except injury, jail or death. The only explanation for not having died yet was either incredible luck or the hand of God. How often did I drive home virtually blind drunk with no care to causing injury to myself or others? Not once was I arrested for DUI (drinking under intoxication) or even stopped. My higher power was watching out for me. Life was messy but fun most of the time, especially after a few pops, but not without tragedy and sadness.

Life went on! Setting up golf games and drinking rendezvous with my alcoholic friends. I thought life was okay. I had enough money coming in to support my lifestyle. After several bad hangovers, I would come to my senses, somewhat, and make every effort to discuss reconciliation with Suzette. My efforts were feeble and any ray of hope to repair our marriage was slowly but surely disappearing. The serpent had me firmly in his clutches of pleasing and satisfying my desires as he occupied my mind constantly. "Where was God in all this?" He was always there by my side—I just did not give Him the time of day; He waited patiently for me to return home someday.

My children were now young adults-the two oldest in college and the two youngest still in high school. Although my life was spent mostly on selfish self-centered ideas, time was somewhat balanced between me and my children. They were and always will be the love of my life. It is quite miraculous that they forgave me later in life, since I frequently chose, while intoxicated with the Serpent, to satisfy my own pleasures rather than theirs. There were so many broken promises, time and time again with disappointment after disappointment. It is a God-given relationship with all of us to have forgiven one another, and for that love for each other to have only grown over the years.

But in spite of all this love and forgiveness I was on that slippery slope of no return that leads to nowhere, except injury, jail or death.

PART TWO

Collapse and Recovery

Chapter 7

The Serpent Dies — the Savior is Born

AUGUST 1, 1986 was an incredibly important day in my life, and I shall never forget it. After working one morning, my buddies and I drove to the famous *Arnold Palmer's Bay Hill Golf Club Resort*. It was a great sunshine day, as we say in sunny Florida (the Sunshine State). What more could I ask for in life than to play golf on this *Thank God Its Friday (TGIF)* day, while drinking throughout the round? My father always warned me, "Never drink during work or on the golf course, and never drink hard liquor. Hard liquor makes big men out of little men." Obviously, I was not an obedient son, and up to this point in my life I had heeded little of what my father tried to teach me. Why start now?

As planned, the day progressed beautifully, and the heavy drinking of afternoon moved right into heavy drinking at the club's 19th hole until late that night but I couldn't tell you a thing that happened that night, as I had another blackout. The next morning came, and I knew I was in trouble. I had the mother-of-all hangovers, and an illness permeated my entire body. I would have given anything to stay and sleep this one off, and I probably would have but, unfortunately, you guessed it, I was separated again and was staying at my boss' house.

Unable to drive because of the shakes, I rode to work with him. After suffering through a brief sales meeting, I struggled with overcoming feelings of desperation and illness, and then it happened. Suddenly, my body started to unravel; my system became inoperative. My mind, heart and total sense of life, seemed to be evaporating. I felt totally helpless; my pulse dropped rapidly. Having gone through pre-med, my manager, Bert, identified the danger immediately and tried to no avail to get juice and crackers down me. Everything in me and around me seemed to be in extra slow motion. Bert loaded me in the car and frantically rushed me to the hospital emergency room. The nurse checked my vitals as I drifted into oblivion, barely hearing the nurse blurt out, "Oh shit, get the doctor. Quick!" The doctor on call immediately assessed my condition and hooked me up to life support. As I lay on the cold gurney, staring up at the ceiling, everything around me turned bright white. I was completely alone at that moment and totally broken sensing the gates of death. My addiction, my great friend, the serpent in disguise had brought me to the brink of death and abandoned me. I was hopelessly lost. I desperately needed someone to be there with me because I was not ready to die. Acutely sensing the edge of death, I cried out aloud for the first time to my Creator and my Lord, "Dear Lord, Help Me!"

I had, at that very moment, totally surrendered to God and asked for His mercy, declaring to live with the promise of never drinking again. The serpent booze, that had been my total dependence and had spewed me out and left me alone hundreds of times, was now suffering the same fate: I spewed him out. I was discovering a new friend, a new dependence, for my life. In that moment, I went from dependence on the serpent, to near death, to new life, and dependence on my savior. From—Serpent to Savior. The words of Jesus learned and remembered from adolescence, my church-going days at Blessed Sacrament Catholic Church, were actually happening while I laid helpless in the E.R., "All who hear and see His word and believe are fully restored as children of God." I didn't know it, but I was being transformed. God was answering my call and my dependence was being transferred from Serpent to Savior. I had no way of knowing then that I was dying to the lure and dependence on the physical world, with all the fiendish serpentine allusions and temptations stemming from the bottle. Now experiencing a new life in God and His promises, it was like shedding my old skin and being dressed in a new one.

I would soon learn that unlike deceptive booze abandoning me in my darkest hour, my Savior would never leave me. God would not lie to me or abandon me; He would never leave my side. I would learn that God seemed absent in my life only when I moved away from Him. As long as I kept my eyes fixed on the Lord, I would be Ok.

Out of seduction of the serpent and its darkness came the true and glorious light of my Savior, although not yet visible and not quite accessible. I had one of God's greatest gifts: Hope. The lowest point of my life in the emergency room, coming ever so close to death, marked the beginning of a new relationship with my God, my Savior. He became the apex of my life. My brush with physical death catapulted me into a spiritual birth. In a sense, I would die to myself and rise anew as another person in Christ, a person totally in surrender and dependent on God alone. This was not just another infamous or memorable day of my life; this is the day I nearly died, the day I stopped drinking, and the day I surrendered to my Lord, my God, my Savior—it was August 2, 1986, a date I will never forget.

Throughout my childhood and into half of my life, my Savior had been more of an abstract entity, one to be feared. Eventually, I would choose to spend the other half of my life with the Lord by my side. That inaugurating day in the hospital, I found and experienced a new belief that I could grow in the light of Jesus—a loving and protective Lord. And if called upon, He, His Father, and the Holy Spirit would answer.

After few days of recuperation, I learned my condition was diagnosed as acute hypoglycemia. Throughout the day, I would experience attacks of plummeting blood sugar and go into semi-shock by becoming lightheaded and disoriented. Shakes, sweats and extreme hunger accompanied a general sense of desperation, as it had in my perilous hospital state of near death, which in turn caused radical hyperventilation, a condition that rendered me incapable of carrying out my work duties, or any kind of conversation, when in the midst of the attack. My pulse would drop drastically, sending me into semi-consciousness. Most often, eating helped to stabilize my condition.

One afternoon, another dark cloud arose engulfing me. Sensing the onset of the hypoglycemic symptoms, I stopped my car at the nearest ATM machine so I could buy some food. As I hurriedly approached the ATM machine, a woman in front of me was fumbling with her card not knowing how to work the machine. When the woman repeatedly could not get her card to work, I became more anxious and began to hyperventilate. Realizing my dilemma, I ran into the grocery store next door. Frantically looking for the orange juice counter, I grabbed a half quart of O.J., ripped the top open, and with great relief guzzled it down. Slowly and thankfully, I came back to near normal. In walking to the checkout with an empty O.J. carton, I explained my problem to the cashier, and with accommodation, I was authorized to get some money from the ATM and come back to pay my bill—I was learning to be ruthlessly honest as they say in A.A. and did not even know it yet.

Life seemed so full of surprises, and another life-changing opportunity in disguise happened the next day at work.

Chapter 8

From Hopelessness to Blind Faith

AT THIS JUNCTURE in my life, I was about to physically hit what is called rock bottom. As bad as things were something more was about to dramatically alter my life. Early one morning, sitting in my office in the isolated building away from the rest of the sales force, I sat alone dejected and frightened, because I realized my life was pretty much messed up and I really wasn't sure if it would ever return to any resemblance of normalcy.

I suddenly sensed another attack coming on, and in desperation, I rushed out to breakfast in hopes that eating would quell the attack. Ordering quickly, I waited in what seemed an eternity for the food to arrive.

Although I started eating immediately, it was too late, and my condition worsened. Frantically devouring the rest of the food in hope of a miracle, the black cloud closed around me and I was left defenseless. My mind was in an unfolding nightmare and the food did not help. For the second time in my life, I felt I was losing my mind and on the brink of insanity. My head was exploding as I experienced the approaching cliffs of despair.

I was feeling virtually helpless and totally hopeless. Groping for anything or anyone, I staggered out of the café, not knowing what to do or where to go. I felt the desperate urge to stay on the move, worried that if I stood still, I would lose my mind. In these early stages of recovery, not even knowing it, I had hit a physical rock bottom. Getting into my car, I desperately drove aimlessly down the highway in hopes of regaining my sanity before losing my mind or worse, dying.

I caught sight of a hand-written sign that read ODAT A.A. Led by some inner directive, I swerved right pulling into the drive where somehow my eyes focused on the arrow pointing to the meeting. I came upon a little shack-like structure, and as I pulled over, I noticed people around the building with others getting out of their cars walking into this shack. Slowly and unsure, I got out of my car and entered the shack. My body followed , and before I realized it, I had entered the meeting without consciously realizing what I had done—I had joined an

Alcoholics Anonymous meeting in progress.

I witnessed people embracing each other, some shaking hands, some smiling, and some looking downcast, but all seemed to be drinking coffee. At that moment, a man identifying himself as Bob greeted me at the door and told me to come on in. Again, I felt like I was being led by some inner directive and the situation seemed surreal. Throughout the meeting, my feelings ranged from fear of the unknown, to the sensation of entering uncharted waters, and eventually to a sense of serenity.

As I slowly scanned the room to see who and what type of people were here, I realized this was a diverse and motley group of characters. Some looked homeless, some were dressed in suits, and surprisingly some were the same drunks I frowned at just a year earlier, when that stupid psychiatrist persuaded me to attend my first A.A. meeting. That was when I thought all these people were below me, as if I definitely did not belong; but here I was again, a year later, without reservation, ready and willing to give up total control, eradicating any thoughts of boozing and partying. I wanted someone there to take control and bring my life back to sanity. I was desperate! But from my surroundings I felt a sliver of peace amid the fear giving me a slight sense of knowing I was finally where I belonged.

During the meeting, someone stood up, announced

her first name and that she was an alcoholic. She told us that if we follow these simple steps and be totally honest with ourselves, we will come to realize a new joy and peace that we had never experienced before. Her smile, laughter, and happiness seemed so distant and so far out of reach for me in my misery. So lost and hopeless, I thought to myself that my case was beyond a doubt an exception, and I had little hope. She talked of the miracles that would happen if we were willing to change. I will never forget my inner response as I listened to her. I wanted to tell her my case was far worse, and it would be truly a miracle if I could be able only to smile once again in my life. I wanted those miracles to happen to me.

I was virtually bankrupted physically and mentally, pretty much financially, and almost spiritually. But as the meeting progressed, I saw a tiny, infinitesimal ray of hope. Maybe, just maybe, these miracles could happen to me. After the meeting concluded, I did not want to leave. I felt safe here; Maybe this would be my sanctuary, my road back to sanity.

As everyone was leaving, Bob, the same man who had greeted me at the door tapped me on the shoulder; he told me not to worry, that it was going to be alright. "Just keep coming back."

His confident presence and assurance buoyed me and gave me a newfound hope and strength. I envisioned a friendship growing, and in the ensuing days, months and years, I would grow close to Big Doctor Bob. He would become a light in my life and brightness for my path. These A.A. rooms that I frowned upon a year prior would become my refuge, my safe haven in the days ahead.

After that first Alcoholics Anonymous meeting, I slept well for the first time in ages, knowing there was a possibility of a new life. The next day, I was anxious to go to yet another meeting. Big Doctor Bob became my mentor/sponsor, and he told me to attend 30 meetings in 30 days. As I listened to him, I knew my case was worse than most and I felt a sense of urgency. I needed many more meetings in less time knowing I was a hard case to crack, so I went to 90 meetings in 30 days. Every day, I went to a 12:00 p.m. noon meeting, a 5:30 p.m. meeting and an 8:00 p.m. meeting.

In the next few weeks, little by little, the miracle of recovery unfolded. Bert my boss detecting a glimmer of sanity in my behavior and knowing my previous prowess as a sales manager reinstated me in another car agency. In my new mindset I was developing a pattern of responsibility towards my duties.

However, all did not go well. I began to experience the first of many bumps in the road, I was rendered unable to perform my managerial duties at work because of unexpected spontaneous episodes of an inability to focus with clients for more than a few minutes. I gave into stress that sent me into an oblivious state of mind and I would momentarily excuse myself, retreating to any place where I could find isolation and seclusion. Soon I became paranoid about confronting clients. For all practical purposes, as a sales manager, I was out-of-business.

I was soon called into the general manager's office. He informed me that I was no longer able to perform my managerial duties and that if I wanted to continue working, my duties would be relinquished and reduced to a salesman only. I went from a large salary to straight commission. My ability to be productive became almost non-existent. I felt I was becoming a spectacle and a distraction to the rest of the sales force. Dejected once more, I packed up my belongings and retreated back to the vacant building, isolated once again from the rest of the sales force. Like dominoes, all the things that I had relied on to function were crumbling before my very eyes.

There was no booze, no deception, and no remedy to pacify myself, except an A.A. meeting. My life was transitioning again into a new routine. I felt powerless to regain my normal well-being—life seemed to just be happening as if I were being dragged along for the ride. My days were spotted with feelings of lightheadedness, acute disorientation, and helplessness. I would begin the day full of hope in regaining my sanity—starting a new life in sobriety. Then by mid-morning, a dark cloud would begin to envelop me. The sense of death at my doorstep would engulf every fiber of my being.

Eventually, after weeks and months of this reclusiveness, the simple functions of living became frighteningly difficult as I lost my confidence. My job became impossible. My earning power vanished to almost the point of bankruptcy. My bills mounted rapidly, and as the old Irish adage says, "When the Wolf is at the Door, Love goes Out the Window." This was true for me. This disease called alcoholism was beating me down. Thank God for the A.A. program. The meetings of Alcoholics Anonymous were my godsend; the meetings buoyed me during these tumultuous changing times.

My wife and I tried to patch things up, but to no avail. She wanted no part of a drunk who was financially, emotionally, and physically bankrupt. Worse yet, I was unable to perform sexually. Our marriage was teetering on bankruptcy, at the very least. She had had enough. There I was alone physically, financially, and almost spiritually bankrupt, yet little did I know that God firmly held onto me. That small decision made in a split-second months before in the emergency room would forever change my life, a desperate cry for help was being answered. Three times a day God would guide me into the doors of A.A. meetings, and all three times, I would listen to the stories of people desperate just like me, telling of their hopeless addiction and how they turned everything over to the will of God. The only thing I had to do was to take a necessary simple step. "One day at a time," as I heard explained repeatedly.

First, I had to accept the fact that I was an alcoholic. Then I had to admit that my life had become totally unmanageable. My newfound fellowship declared, "That if you seek God, He can and will…." I thought this sounded too easy to be true, until my sponsor told me there was one hitch. "This program is a program of action, not just 'a hope and a prayer,'" he said. "You have to do your part."

As I went through the 12-Steps, my spiritual well-being was becoming stronger, and as a result, I began to dream once again, to think more positively.

Step 1. We admitted we were powerless over alcohol- that our lives had become unmanageable.

Step 2. Came to believe that a Power greater than ourselves could restore us to sanity.

Step 3. Made a decision to turn our will and our lives over to the care of God as we understood Him.

Step 4. Made a searching and fearless inventory of ourselves.

Step 5. Admitted to God, to ourselves, and to another human being the exact nature of our wrongs.

Step 6. Were entirely ready to have God remove all these defects of character.

Step 7. Humbly asked Him to remove our shortcomings.

Step 8. Made a list of all persons we had harmed and became willing to make amends to them all.

Step 9. Made direct amends to such people wherever possible, except when to do so would injure them or others.

Step 10. Continued to take personal inventory and when we were wrong promptly admitted it.

Step 11. Sought through prayer and meditation to improve our conscience contact with God, as we understood Him, praying only for knowledge of His will for us and the power to carry that out.

Step 12. Having had a spiritual awakening as the results of these steps, we tried to carry this message to alcoholics, and to practice these principles in all our affairs.

As I WORKED these 12 Steps, I began to have faith that things could happen even to me. I might even find joy in my life, and maybe I could even smile again.

A great lesson in faith happened one evening when I picked up a fellow alcoholic, Blind Bernie, and his seeing-eye dog, for an 8:00 p.m. meeting. It was a great lesson for me of completely turning a problem over to the care of God. The Alcoholics Anonymous meeting concluded at 9:00 p.m., and as usual everyone socialized with a cup of coffee afterwards. Everyone seemed to know Bernie, and it seemed that he talked to everyone with me by his side. One by one, people left, and we closed the building with 3-4 people left behind to help do clean-up service; A.A. encourages doing service whenever possible. We were advised to leave the place as we found it.

It began to rain, a real downpour as we exited the shack. I ushered Bernie and his dog out to the field where the car was parked. We were all drenched—Bernie and I and the dog, who shook all over us once we were in the car out of the rain. As I started the engine and began to move forward, I realized the car was quickly sinking in the sugar sand. Fear engulfed me instantly.

There we were, at 10:00 p.m. in a torrential rainstorm, and my tires were submerged in sugar sand. I had no money and my newly found friends, Blind Bernie and his seeing-eye dog, were in the car with me. Thankfully, there were still two people that had not left the building. Both came over to assist us with our situation. One had a light chain and the other had a small rope. In my assessment of the choices, the chain seemed most likely to work, while the rope had not a chance of helping us. As I shared my optimism with Blind Bernie, he responded confidently. "Do not worry, God will take care of us." This was easy for him to say, as he was not driving. I thought to myself, "I am drenched in pouring rain, I am broke, and I have Blind Bernie and his wet stinking dog in my car."

Our first attempt was with the chain. We tied it on my front bumper to the other car's rear bumper, and on the count of three, everyone pushed from behind. Taking no more than a split second, the chain snapped. Just as I had suspected it would. "We" really have a major problem now." I said to myself. The only thing left was the skinny rope.

Again, Bernie reiterated confidently, "Don't worry Bill; God will take care of it. Everything will be okay."

As I tied the rope to the bumpers, whispering to myself negatively, "This is not going to work," I began thinking ahead, "What is my next option. What am I going to do with Blind Bernie and his dog?" On three, altogether, we pushed the car. In my skepticism, I remarked, "No, it can't be. The car is moving out of the sugar sand like it was on a dry pavement." I looked at the rope after we got out, thinking to myself, "Impossible."

As I got back in the car to drive away, Bernie said softly, "I told you God would take care of everything." As I drove away, totally relieved, I wondered to myself, *Did Bernie really believe God would take care of it?*

Only later, after years of faith formation, would I realize that scripture reading was teaching me to trust God as much as Bernie did. I was remembering the scripture of Blind Bartimaeus as he sat yelling out, "Jesus! Son of David! Have mercy on me!" Meanwhile the skeptical followers, and even Apostles, were relentlessly calling out, "Be Quiet!"

Jesus asked Bartimaeus, "What do you want me to do for you?"

Bartimaeus answered, "I want to see again."

Jesus told him, "Go, your faith has made you well." (Mark 10:47-52)

It was Blind Bernie's faith that trusted God to get us out of the sandy bog, and for the first time ever, I witnessed someone who had total trust and belief in their God or as A.A. says, a higher power. For the first time, I was able to look beyond my sorry predicament and realized that there is without a doubt a God that could and would come to my rescue if I simply wanted to believe and would ask Him to do so. Blind Bernie gave me faith, trust and belief that the Lord is in charge, as I began to ask God more often for His help—I even began to expect results.

In the following weeks, as I went through the A.A. 12 Steps with my sponsor, Big Doctor Bob, my emotional, mental, physical and spiritual well-being grew stronger. I began believing that my dreams could still come true. Little by little, day by day, things began to get better. As I worked my own program, more little things began to happen unexpectedly that helped build my faith. Like Blind Bernie's resolve that God would bring us out of the sugar sand, my own small faith experiences began happening more often as I asked God for His help; I even began to expect positive results from the Lord. God was taking charge of my life, as I let Him.

BEATITUDES

"Happy are those who know they are spiritually poor.

The Kingdom of heaven belongs to them!

Happy are those who mourn; God will comfort them!

Happy are those who are Humble; They will receive what God has promised!

Happy are those whose greatest desire is to do what God requires;God will satisfy them fully!

Happy are those who are merciful to others; God will be merciful to them!

Happy are the pure in heart; They will see God!

Happy are those who work for peace; God will call them his children!

Happy are those who are persecuted because they do what God requires;The Kingdom of heaven belongs to them!

Happy are you when people insult you and persecute you and tell all kinds of evil lies against you, because you are my followers.

Be happy and glad, for a great reward is kept for you in heaven.

Matthew 5:3-11

Chapter 9

Risking Change by Faith Alone

MEANWHILE AT WORK, out of the goodness of my manager and his big heart, rather than being fired, I was moved to an isolated building so I could be by myself. I had reached rock bottom. Multiple daily attacks were common in my anxiety and withdrawal from alcoholism. I was having both hypoglycemic and panic attacks.

An insurance man visited the car dealership where I was working, and he talked to me about the possibility of a career in insurance. Though my health was poor, this opportunity restored my confidence and faith, I thought. I studied hard, took the necessary steps, got my state license, and was set to embark on a new career, although it was financially difficult at first. I slowly transitioned into my new career, still remaining at the dealership initially where commissions were virtually none. Without 2 to 3 months of income in reserve, I had to work both careers, working my old job half-heartedly. I was serving two masters at the same time. That proved to be less than faithful and not fruitful for either business. I began to stress out even more, making my anxiety worse.

Then one day out of the clear blue a friend, Pat, I had not seen in years, walked into my office. As I explained my health dilemma to him, I noticed a grin on his face, a grin that eventually grew into laughter. I was somewhat dismayed by his amusement. He looked at me and joyfully unfolded his own story of how he battled the same condition, only his was worse. Pat proceeded to say that I would be all right and not to worry. His words echoed Big Dr. Bob's from my first A.A. meeting. Pat's story was powerful in the sense that I, too, could overcome this condition, my disease of alcoholism. I began discovering that my Savior was coming to rescue me through other people-some of them recovering alcoholics. This whole business working the steps was not only about me, but was also about reaching out to others.

During all my alcoholic years, it was all about me – who I could manipulate, how many possessions I could amass, and how much power and self-pleasure I could attain, and as long as I was in-charge, I could control things.

This newfound dependence on God, this surrender of me to Him was counter to all that I was before A.A. I was developing a thirst and hunger to know more and more about Our Savior, Jesus Christ. Daily study of the A.A. big book, the A.A. Black Book of daily meditations, and the Holy Bible began to increase my faith and knowledge; my studies began to form a new heart within me. I began to form a true vision of God's purpose for me on earth. What His will was for me here began to become clear to me though I was not always perfect in understanding or executing it.

As my earning power declined, financial pressure and instability caused extreme problems in my marriage. On and off separation and liquidation of my real estate to save my marriage failed terribly. Finally, through the advice of my wife's Lutheran pastor, we dissolved our marriage. For the next two years, I would not have any female companionship. I worked strictly on my recovery and rebuilding my health and relationship with God.

I also began to nurture a close relationship with my friends Pat and his wife Mona, and things began to improve. They were truly a godsend during these two years of recovery. They housed me for a few weeks until I was able to find a place and, basically nursed me back to health. Slowly my mind, body and spirit regained their strength and I began to heal. As my confidence slowly returned, I continued to read scripture and attended A.A.

meetings, as my knowledge of Our Lord increased.

One Friday night, Pat took me to a Bible study at the house of a friend. We sang songs and studied the scripture, and that night left an indelible imprint on my mind and soul. The titillating notion of growing closer to Jesus, His charisma of love, intensified within me. I had a hunger to learn more about my Savior and to know Him more intimately. Pat told me of a priest, Fr. Patrick Caverly, a friend he had known for 30 years, a holy man with a seemingly direct pipeline to God. He asked if I would like to meet with him for personal reconciliation (confession, as I recalled and understood it from my childhood as a Catholic). I had mixed emotions about meeting with the Catholic priest, because of my guilt over having been away from the Church for so long and my guilt of addiction and sins. A.A. Steps 3-7 are to examine all of your past sins, make reparation, ask forgiveness of those whom you have injured or harmed, as well as forgiving those who have harmed you. Pat's suggestion seemed like the best way for me to work these steps.

Then one night, I had a yearning to get involved with the Catholic Church and to attend mass again. I felt it was the missing link in my life that had been absent from much of the past 25 years. On the other hand, I had a feeling of trepidation, probably brought on by the deep shame and guilt I had over my past ways of life.

I finally consented to reconciliation and Pat said he

would arrange to go with me to see the priest the following week. I was out of town on business early that week, but anxiously awaited this meeting anticipating its wonderful cleansing and purification. Wednesday night before the meeting, Pat called saying, "I have good news and bad news." Father Caverly is excited about meeting with you on Saturday at 10:00 a.m." Then came the bad news. "I cannot be there with you but not to worry, Father said to tell you reconciliation will be painless."

Saturday morning arrived quickly, and the priest was warm and easy to talk to. He asked if I was prepared for reconciliation, and I said, "Yes." I recalled how confession used to be and how I was accustomed to it for over 15 years as an adolescent.

"Reconciliation is open now, face-to-face." He said. A streak of fear grabbed me. I was expecting a dark confessional with a screen separating us where I could remain anonymous and confess my sins. But confessing all my past sins face-to-face was scary. He assured me again that it would be painless, and nothing I could say would shock him.

Father Caverly calmed my nervousness, as I thanked the Lord. He was right. It was painless! My realization of this cleansing and purification happened almost instantly for me. I felt a huge burden removed from my shoulders, and I instantly had a giant thirst to know everything there was to know about the Church, God and Jesus, my

Shepherd and Savior.

Ironically, this reconciliation was the miracle that freed me from my guilt and shame; this confession was my working steps four through ten of the Alcoholics Anonymous Program, and it began to have an effect. It allowed me to make a fearless and searching moral inventory of myself. I admitted to God the exact nature of my wrongdoings. I asked God to remove all these defects of character and burden I had carried all these years. I began to list all the people I had harmed and was willing to make amends to them all. I contacted some of the people where I could and tried not to hurt the people I once loved. I continued through regular confession to examine my sins, and if injuring anyone emotionally, mentally or spiritually, I promptly admitted it. The more I worked on this cleansing, the more I shed my shame, guilt, self-deprecation, and fear, regaining my confidence by completing these steps.

My sins were like cataracts that blurred my vision of who God wanted me to be. As I slowly regained my vision without alcohol, seeing clearly again, my life had incredible possibilities, and I had a future once again. My state of mind changed to one of peace and tranquility as I found laughter within me once again, and I began to dream once more.

From this point, the fast-track to put my life back to normal became my priority. My life actually had balance again-balance among family, spirituality, work, and play. Weekly church attendance, confession and A.A. meetings were important to keep me moving in the right direction. I began sharing more time with my family. I set financial goals and as I reached to attain them they began to unfold. My play time was weekly golf with friends and family. Most importantly, something else would consume me for the remainder of my life-the miracle that was about to unfold!

Chapter 10

Prayer works — New Beginning

FR. CAVERLY, MY new church pastor, suggested that I get involved in one of the many ministries such as feeding the poor or visiting the sick. The program he suggested was the RCIA ministry (Right of Christian Initiation of Adults) that refers to the process where an adult is introduced to the Roman Catholic faith. In this program, I would learn of the creation of Adam and Eve to the birth of Christianity, and how it relates to me presently. Also, in this program, I would sponsor someone interested in entering the Catholic Church and becoming a member of the faith. Although the program would take almost a year of formation, I was thrilled at the opportunity and thought of helping someone else draw closer to our Savior.

Fr. Caverly then introduced me to a religious nun in our community, Sr. Theresa Mary Dolan, Head of the adult spirituality program, and the RCIA ministry. She was very gracious and gave me two books to read, *Christ Among Us* by Anthony Wilhelm, and *Believing in Jesus* by Leonard Foley. This is not a proselytization attempt to convert anyone to Catholicism, but merely a conveyance of the events that took place in my recovery. It wasn't long after I started the RCIA program that I realized when studying that there were two major changes in my thought patterns: 1) my heart was open for a new journey in faith, and 2) my heart was open to meet someone to take this incredible journey with me. It had been almost two years since I had dated or had any relationship with a woman.

Then one night at the home of my friends Pat and Mona, I confided in them that I was ready to have another relationship. That night lying in bed, the idea came back to me, and I felt something stir within my heart as I prayed asking God to send me a soul mate. I prayed for someone I could grow spiritually with, and I was convinced God would answer my prayer, if it be His will. I even asked if He would make her a five-handicap golfer—someone I could love, grow with and enjoy God's greatest invention, golf. I guess my natural salesmanship kicked in. Oh well. After all, He did say, "Ask and it will be given to you; Seek and you will find; Knock and the door will be opened to you." The response was a beatific vision or epiphany of some sort. I had no vision or voice but sensed God responding. God whispered in my mind not to worry and that He would soon send me His gem to journey with. Though I didn't actually hear a voice, the words and message were irrefutably clear.

The next night I drove to the church to attend a ministry talk called Divorce Recovery, a support group for those either divorced, contemplating a divorce, or in the process of getting a divorce. I arrived at my first meeting a little late. Inadvertently, I opened the wrong door and entered the room near the podium that meant I was facing the whole group. As soon as I entered the room, my eyes met another set of eyes in the audience that would have the greatest impact on my life. My heart leapt with joy when I laid eyes on her. I was stunned by her beauty. Although seated during the whole meeting, I was deaf to the talk of the speaker; my mind raced to figure out how I could meet this radiant and stunning woman. As the meeting ended, everyone gathered into a circle to pray the 'Lord's Prayer' all joining hands, and to my surprise, the hand that clasped mine was that of this incredible woman. Grasping her hand was a titillating experience, and I couldn't wait to introduce myself afterwards.

The prayer ended, and another woman walked up and introduced herself to me dominating the few precious moments I thought I had to strike up a conversation with this amazing woman. Before I could look around, she had disappeared from sight. Everyone announced that they were leaving for the pizza parlor social. As I scanned the hallway, there was no sign of my stunning woman and, dismayed, I drove to the pizza parlor hoping for my first opportunity to meet her there. At the pizza parlor, I surveyed the group, but she was nowhere in sight. Disappointed, I left the social.

No sooner had I walked out the parlor door, however, when the beautiful lady drove up to the restaurant. Confused as to what to do, I was thinking I had to move fast, when she pulled up alongside of me to inquire if this was where everyone was meeting. I confirmed this was the place and bashfully introduced myself as she told me her name was Meg. Reluctantly, I told her that I was not staying but did not want to lose the opportunity to visit with her. I gave her my business card and said I would look forward to seeing her again. Off I drove, giggling, and realizing she was even more beautiful face-to-face, and her somewhat low sultry voice simply paralyzed me. I was smitten for sure.

Finally, home at Pat and Mona's, I told my story to them, and they were elated by my electrifying encounter. As I rested for the night, I could not get Meg out of my mind, and began praying and thanking God for all my blessings. As I began to meditate, I thanked the good Lord for possibly bringing a new woman into my life; I thanked Him for my meeting this new woman; and I prayed that she could be my one soul mate. In my silence, I heard again the whisper in the recesses of my heart, a soft voice saying, "Why did you worry? I sent you my gem to be with you." Kaboom! It hit me. God said He would send me His gem, and Gem spelled backwards is Meg. Someone once told me there are no coincidences, and God has a sense of humor too.

Morning came and I was off to work dreaming of my next encounter with Meg, my gem. I went out-of-town on business for the week, feeling like the week would never end. It did and Meg was again at the church group meeting. This time at the conclusion of the meeting, I made sure to communicate with her. We met up at the restaurant where the group was convening. We sat together and the conversation was too good to be true, almost like it was drawn up by some higher power for us to be together.

We made arrangements to meet and play tennis later that week, and throughout the match, my excitement grew. Meg was beautiful beyond words, athletic, and an excellent tennis player. I thought of my mother who was a tennis champion in New England. During our match, I kept hoping how great it would be for her to meet my mother. I thought to myself, "This is too good to be true." Tennis concluded, and we sat and talked for what seemed like hours. Was God answering my prayer to send someone to journey with me, spiritually.

Over the next few weeks, our relationship blossomed and would grow feverishly. After only a few dates, I discovered that God did answer my prayers for the gem I so desired. He did not send me a five-handicap as Meg did not play golf, but that was no longer important. Instead, God sent me not a 10 but a 12-off- the-scale person. Her beauty and her spirituality were beyond anything I could have imagined. We soon became soul mates and would immerse ourselves into several church ministries. She even moved toward the golf proficiency I had so rashly included on my wish list with God.

Meg, active and competitive, soon became interested in learning how to play golf. No sooner said I then drove her to meet my mother, Mary, a champion amateur athlete in city and state with prowess in tennis, basketball and golf. They instantly hit it off and for the next 4-5 years, under my mother's tutelage, Meg grew to become quite the enthusiastic golfer. Every Wednesday Meg would drive to my mother's, pick her up for lunch, and then they would play afternoon golf together. They remained great friends until my mother's passing on St. Patrick's Day 1992.

Over the next two years, I continued to aid in the

RCIA ministry. It was a journey of learning to love God's creation, the story of Genesis as told in the Old Testament through the New Testament, in developing a relationship with Our Savior, Jesus Christ, while helping others grow in faith as well. My study of scripture during this period grew steadily, and my pastor impacted me more so during one of his homilies at mass when he quoted, "If we are ignorant of scripture, we deny Christ."

Incidentally, my new life in Christ was impacting my new life in sobriety that showed great benefits and rewards of the promised miracles. Recognizing there were common roots in both, my journey in sobriety supported my faith journey, for I began to see and think more clearly, and the fog began to lift.

This new found attitude, together with Meg, soon propelled us into another new outreach activity. Ginger, a fellow parishioner, introduced us to a ministry called The Coalition to The Homeless. Each month, we picked up a load of food and brought it to a shelter to feed 500-600 homeless people, men, women and children. Helping the homeless would carry-through still to today in various ways, for we soon learned that it is in giving that we receive. The miracle was truly evolving within me. I was being transformed from a creature obedient to the sins of the serpent to a creature obedient to the love and hope of my creator and Savior. The transformation, however, was a baffling experience in many ways, and I wondered,

"How could this happen." All I could do was, "Go with the flow," as the saying goes, and the flow was falling in love first with God and then Meg given to me by Him.

It turned out that Meg had the same ancestry as myself, Irish, and when I say Irish, I mean fiercely Irish. What a paradox in full circle, and how happy my parents would be to know that, after two false starts, my soul mate is Irish like both of them. Although I think they know somehow as they look down upon us from heaven, finally knowing that their preaching was finally producing something good in me. For certain, though the Irish are well known for alcoholism, it is Meg, whose unconditional love has helped keep me sober. There was only one other fiercely Irish woman in my life, my mother, Mary Ellen Malone O'Connell Mitchell, and of course, my grandmothers who, with my grandfathers, emigrated from Ireland to the United States in the 1890s.

Meg and I are two generations removed from the old sod, namely Eire (the Gaelic name for Ireland). We shared gratitude and love for our Roman Catholic faith, which began with our Irish ancestors over 1600 years ago when St. Patrick, the Bishop of Ireland, introduced Christianity, converting a practicing society of Celtic polytheism, and becoming the revered patron saint of Ireland. That gratitude and love for our faith is filled with love for our Irish ancestors, who through perseverance and persistence in keeping the faith over all these centuries regardless of enduring a litany of catastrophic events. These included the Normandy invasion in 1169 and Henry II's claim over the whole of Ireland in the century. Add to this the shameful injustice of the Penal Laws, laws passed against Roman Catholics in Britain and Ireland after the Reformation that penalized the practice of the Roman Catholic religion and imposed civil disabilities on Catholics. It got even worse with the various acts passed in the sixteenth and seventeenth centuries prescribing fines and imprisonment for participation in Catholic worship and severe penalties, including death, for Catholic priests who practiced their ministry in public. Priests had to celebrate Holy Mass in hiding, in clandestine environments called Mass Rocks. Mass set up in valleys and dells with sentries looking out for British soldiers. Once on a trip to Ireland in County Sligo I came upon such a dell and a Mass rock with this inscription on it:

It has been made holy, by the feet of generations,

Who came to worship God,

To hear Mass, to honor our lady,

To pray for their needs and for peace,

Here are memories of a poor people, persecuted people,

They braved death to come,

They walked barefoot through the woods,

To worship in secret,

Here are the memories of hunted priests,

Offering Mass in this hallowed place,

At the risk of their lives,

Will their sufferings and sacrifices be in vain?

They have handed us a torch,

Let us keep that torch alight.

THE BRITISH CRUELTY continued until the Irish War of Independence (a.k.a. Black and Tan War) beginning in 1919 and ending with the Anglo-Irish Treaty signed on 6 December 1921. The 26 counties of Southern Ireland seceded from the Protestant north of six counties that remain loyal to England to this day.

The honor and thankfulness for the gift of faith to us soon turned into a pilgrimage to our ancestral land. Upon arriving in the land of forty shades of green, we proudly visited each town our grandparents were born in. This would turn into a real love affair with both the country of Ireland and its people. We also fell in love with the pub life, always abuzz with traveling musicians and of course the Guinness flowing. My sobriety withstood the test of the Irish pubs, and I became the designated driver. I did enjoy seeing Meg partake in a pint or two and join in the merriment and craic (Pronounced crack and meaning for the Irish, "high-spirited fun in the serious work of play"). Even though I was probably one of the few people in the pub that did not drink, I felt my sobriety was a blessing not only for me but, for all my ancestry that couldn't shake the habit they called "The Drink." I felt I was carrying the torch for all of them as well.

Chapter 11

Miracle of Mercy
Compassion – Forgiveness

IN THE TWO years of my newfound sober life, mostly 1987, two things would be learned and experienced as God's great gifts, which I would carry with me for the rest of my life: Forgiveness and Love. I had to learn to ask for forgiveness, learn how to receive forgiveness and most importantly, forgive those that in any way hurt me. St. Augustine, the great 4th century Catholic Saint, wrote several books, including one that has influenced and changed the hearts of millions worldwide called Confessions, which outlines his sinful youth and conversion to Christianity and Catholicism. Augustine once said, "God is always trying to give good things to us, but our hands are too full to receive them." I realized that it meant that it was virtually impossible to forgive someone if you have not forgiven yourself. Often times, our guilt blocks us from reaching out to God to forgive us. Our hands remain too full.

To love someone else you must fully love yourself. The forgiveness that I realized and experienced was between not only my children whom I had abandoned most of their life, growing up with broken promises, but also my ex-wife, mother of our children. It's as if all the hate and all of the resentment had evaporated as I completed the Alcoholics Anonymous 12 Steps. What remained when I surrendered was only love that was lit aglow with hope of having the good life. I would in the next several years grow and develop a more intimate relationship and friendship with my children. I often pondered how this forgiveness, this miracle came about.

I soon realized that it came about by me taking the first step to ask for forgiveness; and in the first step, I had to humble myself, especially with my children and ex-wife. It was through writing letters to the people I harmed in my past that I began my reparation. The process was summed up in doing Steps 4 and 5. Step 4 says, "Make a searching and fearless moral inventory of ourselves", and Step 5 says, "Admit to God, to ourselves and to another human being the exact nature of our wrongs."

Over the ensuing months of working the A.A. 12

Steps, things were good, life was good, and I began to know Christ, the focus of my new life. It would take several years for me to fully realize the greatest gift of all, forgiveness and love—the miracle that was promised.

Soon after beginning my recovery with A.A., with renewed purpose and energy, I founded my own insurance business, studying and completing the required courses and taking the State board exam to become licensed both as an agent as well as an agency. Through connections I had with other agencies I was introduced to Guy Norberg, also in the insurance business. Through Guy's tutelage direction and advice my business took off. We also developed a close spiritual relationship that has lasted till this day. The business grew with each step and each year and soon thereafter availed Meg and me opportunities to travel worldwide together. But with all the blessings received from my change in recovery, it did not erase entirely my many defects of character. These would slowly be erased only with the help of God over time and on His timetable, not mine.

I constantly had to remind myself that I was still on thin ice as far as my sobriety was concerned. I knew I couldn't let my guard down because of the insidiousness of alcoholism. I had the sense that the serpent was still waiting in the wings, hoping I would carelessly make another foolish decision like I did that Christmas in 1985 that started with "Have just one drink." Keenly aware of this potential disaster, I continued to attend nightly A.A. meetings to keep fresh in my mind what I have to do to remain sober. I was a broken person and had to remind myself that it would take an undeterminable amount of time to heal and to strengthen myself.

I was only too aware that action was required on my part to complete the change from vulnerability to the serpent to dependence instead on my Savior Jesus, and his promises of peace, joy and love here on earth, and the ultimate eternal life with Him. Just one drink away from becoming a drunk again, I chose to continue two things that would assure my sobriety: To attend as many A.A. meetings as possible, and to pray to the almighty Lord giving Him thanks. Not only did I attend A.A. meetings, but I began attending Sunday Mass every week, just like my father. (We really do become more like our parents as we age.) When possible, I would also attend a daily noon Mass at least twice a week. Not coincidentally I am sure, the A.A. program that catapulted me out of the gutters of misery and hopelessness had steps that mirrored life as a practicing Catholic Christian and my own faith-filled upbringing as well.

Let me be clear before I continue. When I say Catholic Christian, I am not excluding all other Christian denominations or even non-denominational, nor Hindu, Buddhist, Islam, Jewish, or any other sect or religion, even non-believers. I think the make-up of that Supreme

Being or higher power is a Spirit of unconditional love. So, I can say with all certainty that this God even loves deeply those who do not believe—along with all people of all races and all believers everywhere. So, let us proceed! Whether we are believers or non-believers, keeping an open mind of course, all people are sacred, a gift from a Creator greater than ourselves. God created each and every one of us in His likeness and love. That makes all of us children of God, as well as brothers and sisters to the good Lord and to one another. I would say that our human thinking and interpretation of life is what has separated us and created chasms, roadblocks and walls that stymie and block what we were created for in the first place, to share His unconditional love with one another.

Allow me to describe how the Alcoholics Anonymous 12 Step program mirrors the faith journey that came from my own personal experience of working the 12-step program and the correlation with my Roman Catholic faith.

The best way for me to describe the 12 steps is to review my own healing and recovery as it was reflected and mirrored through my faith journey, which is preceded by my own personal experience rooted in the Roman Catholic faith. Although the process and the results of the 12 steps mirrored Catholicism for me, the faith built into the program is fashioned and formed in spirituality that belongs to most all denominations of faith. To me, the 12 steps of Alcoholics Anonymous is a fellowship of addicts practicing the principle of regaining love of themselves and learning to love mankind unconditionally, all ensconced within and hidden in the principals of Christianity. Alcoholics Anonymous was created in 1935 by Bill Wilson and Dr. Bob Smith, both suffering alcoholics, and one of these two gentlemen was Catholic like me that counseled often with a priest. Today, the program is worldwide, multi-cultural, diverse and has over 2 million members as of this writing.

As you read these 12 steps, heed their meaning wisely and open mindedly, and understand one thing. I have come to understand with all certainty there is no other way to regain your sobriety and sanity. Countless alcoholics have tried other ways but have ultimately failed. I believe there is no other way! You have no other choice. So, let us begin. Here are the 12 steps as the two A.A. founders wrote them.

> **Step 1** » **"We admitted we were powerless over alcohol that our lives had become unmanageable."** Whatever state of mind we are experiencing at any given time in our life, whether grief, shame, hopelessness, anger, fearfulness, complacency, self-righteousness to name a few, we cry out for healing knowing we possess these defects.

STEP 2 » **"Came to believe that a power greater than ourselves could restore us to sanity."** As a Catholic, the God that created me and you, that is seen and unseen and who formed us in the image and likeness of Himself, gave us life to do His will and can and will reshape our lives bringing love to the forefront of our true purpose in life, if we allow Him.

STEP 3 » **"Made a decision to turn our will and our lives over to the care of God as we understood Him."** As a Christian, we can decide to courageously enter into and return to a relationship with Our Creator, God, through prayer, meditation and quiet time in the silence of our heart. There may not be much silence initially, but the more we pray the more peace we will attain. The Catholic rosary prayer beads are a form of meditation that helps clear the mind and focus on the prayer to our Lord, much like the Tallit in Judaism, the Subha in Islam, and the Japa Mala in Hinduism.

STEP 4 » **"Made a searching and fearless moral inventory of ourselves."** At some point in life, we all go back and look at what we did, what we didn't do, what we could have done, and what we could have done better, wherein lies the guilt of our past. But unless we are willing to exam ourselves, we will remain stuck in our past, making the same mistakes over as we have always done, even without even knowing it. It will not be easy to undo our past, and sometimes we can't undo it, but we can "Let it Go" and go on with our future. It is only when we look deep inside ourselves that we can reveal, expose, acknowledge and unmask our weaknesses. Then and only then can we plead to our maker, our higher power, to become unshackled.

Step 5 » **"Admitted to God, to ourselves and to another human being the exact nature of our wrongs."** The sacrament of reconciliation or confession as we call it in Catholicism is taking and making a list of all shortcomings and transgressions, a.k.a. sinfulness. When we write it down, we are asked to give it away, and it is in relinquishing the sins of our past, we are ready to be cleansed and healed in forgiveness. As a Catholic, we offer our sorrow to God for our sins, and in giving our shortcomings to the priest (giving away all of our inventory), we begin to trust another human being, we trust that God forgives us our inventory with absolution from the good Lord through the intercession of a non-judgmental priest, whereas some may feel more comfortable placing their trust in a non-judgmental sponsor as is suggested in Alcoholics Anonymous.

STEP 6 » **"Were entirely ready to have God remove all these defects of character."** During our Catholic confession/reconciliation, we confidently thirst to have the priest absolve us, believing that the priest is God's called representative here on earth succeeding the twelve Apostles chosen by Jesus Himself – and believing that the Holy Spirit is with the priest during absolution, bestowing upon the recipient God's forgiving grace. No human being can forgive any sin committed against God, but we can forgive another human being. We believe all sin is a violation of God's natural law. Your AA sponsor will gently and confidentially guide you through this step.

STEP 7 » **"Humbly asked Him to remove our shortcomings."** As repenting Catholics, we humble ourselves before the Lord by asking for His forgiveness; we ask for His healing heart and our transformation into the person that He wants and created us to be. Again, your sponsor will tenderly explain this process.

STEP 8 » **"Made a list of all persons we had harmed and became willing to make amends to them all."** We are asked to love our neighbor as ourselves for the love of God. Likewise, in Leviticus 6:1-5, "The Lord gave the following regulations to Moses. An offering is to be made if anyone sins against the Lord by refusing to return what a fellow Israelite has left as a deposit or by stealing something from him or by cheating him or by lying about something that has been lost and swearing that he did not find it. When a man sins in any of these ways, he must repay whatever he got by dishonest means. On the day he is found guilty, he must repay the owner in full, plus an additional 20 percent." Even in Proverbs 16:6-7, it is written, "Be loyal and faithful, and God will forgive your sin. Obey the Lord and nothing evil will happen to you. When you please the Lord, you can make your enemies into friends." Thus, we let go of all inclination to sin of our own selfishness; we surrender our pride and make peace with others for us to be at peace within ourselves.

STEP 9 » **"Made direct amends to such people wherever possible, except when to do so would injure them or others."** We begin thinking first of others than ourselves, and in doing so, we begin to realize the ways that we hurt others. We ask for the Holy Spirit to guide us in His understanding ways so not to cause others any harm. As we make our amends, we are guided by a new conscientiousness of not offending God by offending others. If making amends means offending or hurting others, then we find another way to make the amends, whether it be writing a letter and giving it to our sponsor, or confessing it to a priest, doing a good deed or favor for someone else close to the person or performing an action without them knowing about. There are many different ways we can make amends, and each of us knows best, but this is not to say that mistakes won't be made, and over time with prayer we keep asking for their forgiveness.

STEP 10 » **"Continued to take personal inventory and when we were wrong promptly admitted it."** As part of the Catholic faith, we know that there are no perfect people in this life, and we are all sinners. Even after we have amended with our past, we keep repenting on a day-to-day basis, reviewing what we did good and not so good that day. We continue our new way of life staying in a state of grace of God, Our Creator, Our Maker, Our Savior, and Our Higher Power.

STEP 11 » **"Sought through prayer and meditation to improve our conscious contact with God as we understood Him, praying only for knowledge of His will for us and the power to carry that out."** Through prayer, meditation, attending Mass, going to confession, reading and studying the bible, and the AA Big Book we prioritize our lives by renewing our mind in seeking God first in all things and making Him our sole purpose in life.

Catholic Saint Mother Theresa explained prayer like this:

"The fruit of silence is prayer.

The fruit of prayer is faith.

The fruit of faith is love.

The fruit of love is service.

The fruit of service is peace."

STEP 12 – **"Having had a spiritual awakening as the result of these steps, we tried to carry this message to alcoholics and to practice these principles in all our affairs."** We are commanded to love God with all our heart, with all our mind, with all our strength, with all our soul (heart, body, mind and soul) to grow in love with all His people unconditionally; He commands us to love one another as He loves us. We become seekers of those broken and hopelessly addicted to alcoholism, drugs, sex, gambling, and many other addictions; we bring others to God's loving presence as He will offer them the miracle of Peace, Love and Hope too.

I CAN MORE clearly look at this life and discern what my purpose really is here. The process of recovery was gradual in focusing on what life is really all about and finding the key to unlocking its enormous mystery. Two things in the ensuing months would miraculously happen that would clearly help me in my recovery. I would discover who I am and define my life's purpose.

PART THREE

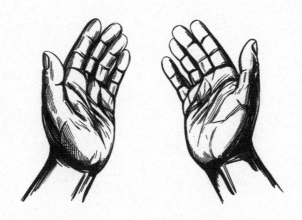

Discovery

Chapter 12

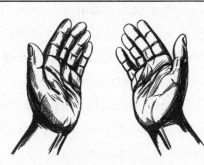

Finding Purpose
Who Am I? — Meaning of Life

BY 1993 THE process of recovery was gradually defining what life is really all about. Two things in the ensuing months would help me more clearly define my life's purpose.

First, I physically collapsed at work one day. As the ambulance came and put me on the stretcher I felt as though life was slowly fading away within me. They hooked me up to life support and rushed me to the hospital. Once in the hospital they immediately assessed the problem as low blood sugar with my blood pressure at dangerously low level and put me on an IV. As I laid there on the cold metal slab, I again had the same eerie feeling of being near death's door—my next breath would be my last.

At that very moment, I had an epiphany, or some would say another unexplainable experience that enveloped me. I envisioned in that precise moment a transition from life to death and a beatific encounter with our Lord Jesus. At that very instant I had a distinct but vague image of Jesus embracing me and clearly saying something to me, without me hearing any words, yet I understood precisely what he was asking me, "How did you love on your life's journey, Bill?"

Immediately I began to weep and was soon blinded by tears. My heart ached in fear that I would not have a chance to say goodbye to Meg and tell her how much I deeply loved her. I also sensed clearly in that moment, an awareness that during my life I had selfishly squandered many opportunities to reach out to those in need with God's Love and His message of Hope.

Obviously, I survived, but the message I received that frightful day would have a profound impact on the rest of my life: Jesus had powerfully helped me put life into perspective. The essence of life was clearly given to me in a new understanding of how and why I am to live my life, and of the brevity and fragility of life itself. My eyes were opened to how life could end in an instant without notice.

Scripture tells us that during the encounter with God that none can escape, He will judge us on how we loved others above anything we may have achieved in life. Jesus gave me a realization that God would use me to spread His Love into the world. He would reach out, see and listen to the cries of the world through me. I had a "Metanoya", meaning a complete change of heart. I remembered the words of Jesus, "When you call me in distress, I hear you and will be with you always."

At the same time, He gave me a tremendous challenge. I wondered how I could live up to the task. Like the twelve Apostles that were sent out to spread the Good News in pairs of two, our Lord would soon bring someone into my life to help spread the word. As the days passed and my health improved, I began to resume the daily activities of my life.

Attending Alcoholics Anonymous meetings, attending Mass, and voraciously delving into scripture and the Big Book of A.A. were priorities. Even when we went out of town on weekends or overseas, we revolved our schedules around Mass on Sundays. Weekly morning Mass once or twice was becoming commonplace in my schedule. In my weekly travels for work in different cities, I found myself stopping for 30 minutes in a nearby church to pray and give thanks to God asking for His strength and forgiveness. In the evenings I would seek out A.A.

meetings. Months passed after my hospitalization and the second life changing event was about to occur. God would again place someone in my life that would change me into a true disciple of my faith and would eventually impact hundreds of people in the years to come, as I learned to share His message of hope and Love.

Sr. Christa Cunningham, a Sinsinawa Dominican sister was the leader of a weekly scripture study at our local Roman Catholic parish, and over the next four years, she would teach me about the story of our faith and the meaning of the Gospel and Good News of our Lord and Savior Jesus. Meg and I both grew together in relationship with God and the mother of our Lord Mary. We grew to thirst for spiritual love from Our Creator, and it began to change my soul from a hardened heart to a person caring for all God's creatures. I immersed myself in fellowship with Christ, and God in turn taught me how to love mankind. Clearly God's Love has no borders and is truly universal. As I began to practice the discipleship of Christ through my faith, my A.A. Step 12 came to fruition by carrying the message of love to others in all my affairs.

By following my Savior, this brought a new challenge to me. By becoming a follower and disciple of Christ, I was called to lead, and this was frightening at first. As time passed, my love for Meg and family grew intensely, with mutual love in relationships with my children, as well as Meg's children, growing into a unified, peaceful and loving family.

God's gift to my reuniting my renewed friendship with Pat and Mona was an integral part of my early recovery beginning 1986 to 1988 and for the first two years helping me solidify my sobriety and finding my faith once again. After Pat helped me make that first confessional appointment my road to recovery from alcoholism sealed my relationship with God and from that point there was no turning back. One night Pat introduced me to a Friday evening bible study with his friend Brian. The evening would begin with the bible study, a sharing period, prayer and singing accompanied by a guitarist; Brian would open with prayer, then different people would recite scripture passages, then open dialog and discussion of the passages, followed by singing. I experienced great joy and felt lifted to a new level of confidence. One Friday evening upon leaving something stirred within my heart, even to the point of evoking me that someday I would like to start my own bible study prayer group. As I left that evening, I had a great sense of peace, joy, love and increased knowledge of God like never before, and somehow it seemed to all fit in this big picture of what God was asking of me in life.

Soon thereafter, I began attending Sr. Christa's frequent adult faith formation programs and bible studies, often led by two Irish priests Fr. Michael Cannon and Fr. Charlie Deeney both born in the same town, Letterkenny, Donegal Ireland. One night in a lecture, Fr. Charlie spoke about the importance of meditating and contemplating God's unconditional love for us, what our purpose in life is, and the gospel message Jesus taught to follow Him in His footsteps, bringing His love and light into the world. And secondly how brief our time is on our earthly journey. Many hundreds of generations have come and gone. Some people in each generation make impacts for the betterment of mankind whether small or significant. Fr. Charlie went on to say, "Time passes. Generations come and go. But each generation starts over in passing down the story of faith and the virtues of our Savior's Love. Right now, this is our moment in time. We are called to try and make a change in the world. Will we let our moment pass or act on it?" This message had a vast impact on how I would look at life from that moment on. How it was my opportunity, challenge, responsibility and command from God to try in some form reach out to those less fortunate and attempt to make a difference. Robert F Kennedy, brother of President JFK, once said, "Some see things as they are and ask, 'why?' I see things as they could be and ask, 'why not?' "

On another night, the parish brought in a panel of people afflicted with Aids. Some had contracted the virus through blood transfusions, others through unsterile needles used by drug addicts, and still others from sexual relationships. Many addicts struggle with HIV as well as alcoholism. After all the panelists spoke someone in the audience sprang up and decried, "Your diseases are a result of God's condemnation." Immediately from the back of the room, Fr. Michael Cannon rose and declared, "Not true. God does not condemn you, but rather embraces you with His Love."

That declaration pierced my heart, mind and soul. God truly does love us unconditionally. None of our sinfulness could possibly transcend His Love for us.

As a Catholic growing up, I did not read the bible, but each time I attended Mass we learned from listening to the Gospel readings, Old Testament readings, Psalms, New Testament readings and then a homily or sermon. So, in the Mass, we were able to comprehend the Holy Scriptures, from both hearing the reading, and then listening to the Priests homily, in which he explained the readings and how they applied to each of our daily lives. I soon discovered that the truths in the Gospel of our Lord and Savior were also found in the 12 steps and the Big Book of A.A.

It is also of utmost importance, when you delve into the Big Book of A.A., that you share your thoughts with your sponsor to make sure your understanding is correct. Likewise, when reading the Holy Scriptures, it is imperative you obtain a commentary that explains the readings, safeguarding you from misinterpreting what you have read. After purchasing my first bible, I joined every bible study I could attend, Catholic and non-Catholic, especially as I just mentioned bible programs held by a Catholic Dominican sister by the name of Sr. Christa, and the young Irish priest, Fr. Michael.

Little by little, I was learning more and more each week of my faith journey encompassing Adam and Eve to Jesus. I was beginning to internalize the Word, to grow and to know my Savior Jesus. I not only wanted to serve Him but was thirsting to follow Him in life by serving others; with each bible study that I attended, each prayer I prayed, each song I sang, each time I attended mass, each time I confessed my sins to the priest, each time I received the Holy Eucharist, it was like being inoculated with the grace, love and spirit of our Lord and Savior. It took about eight years to assimilate my faith as my heart was hungering and soul thirsting for the Lord to consume me.

Finally, in 1995, I decided to begin my own scripture study, following in the footsteps of Jesus. I was ready! First, I examined myself, "Do I have the confidence or courage?" Admittedly by all accounts, it was a weary "Yes." All my life and in most cases, I have lacked the confidence to say "Yes." To me, it is so easy to say, "No" when asked to do something that would require oneself to give up time, talent or money.

As Jesus says, "Whoever would save his life will lose

it, but whoever loses his life for my sake will find it." Again, Jesus said "Greater Love hath no man than this, that a man lay down his life for his friends" (John 15:13). When I first heard theses quotes by Jesus from scripture, I understood them to be physically losing your life as a martyr, but through continuous study of scripture and group discussions, I grew to realize that it also meant dying to oneself through service and work to grow spiritually in order to give our Savior's Love to others.

We each have stories, a defining moment, when someone has touched our lives, and for me, it began with my recovery from alcoholism. We must have the courage and unquestioning faith, belief and hope that Our Savior will transform us. We are all hopeless souls on a journey with our ultimate home in eternal life. We have the choice to choose the darkness of hopelessness or the light of hope, the instrument to a fulfilling life through helping others that still suffer. By helping others, my own recovery was propelled to a new level of love of family and friends, by getting outside of myself and into caring for others. By caring for others, the darkness gradually diminished into a light that allowed me to see with hope, the end of the tunnel, but not without Our Lord's Grace, Strength and Love.

Mother Theresa, another Catholic saint, founded an order called "the Missionaries of Charity." She and her fellow sisters worked with the poorest of the poor in

Calcutta, India. Started by her in 1950, her order today numbers well over 5,000 Sisters worldwide. She once profoundly exclaimed, "If you want to find yourself, lose yourself in the service of others." As you begin to see and relate to others, you relate to yourself in a new way as well. By administering to the afflicted, we give the Christ within us, enabling us to share His love with others. We cannot give what we do not have, but ironically, we receive by giving. By taking the first step of courage to meet others where they are, we take our own step of recovery. In not giving up, you will one day become the one living in the light and may be touching a myriad of others living in hopelessness and darkness.

It is so easy to say, "No," when asked to do something that would require one to give of their time, talent or money. A rich young man came to Jesus and asked him, 'Teacher, what good deed must I do to have eternal life?"

Jesus told him, "If you sell what you have and give to the poor, you will have great treasure in Heaven. Then come, follow me." But when the young man heard this, he went away sad, for he had many possessions.

Chapter 13

Searching for Who God Is

A DEFINING MOMENT in my faith came one Sunday morning in 1995 after attending mass. As Meg and I exited the church, I ran into Sr. Teresa Mary Dolan, who had helped start my faith formation in 1987. Upon sharing with her my desire to start a bible study, she responded saying, "All of us are called at some time to answer the soft prodding within our hearts of Our Lord Jesus saying, "Come Follow Me." We have a choice to respond by saying, 'Yes, I will Lord" or "No, not now Lord" and move on. She said she was certain that I was ready to say "Yes."

At that moment I remembered Fr. Charlie saying,

"This is our moment in time."

No sooner had I said goodbye to Sister than my Nigerian friend, Lawrence Chukwu, came walking out. We had attended numerous scripture studies together over the years. I nervously greeted him, asking if he would be interested in starting a bible study with me and Meg. I was prepared and expecting Lawrence to probably say no, but was overwhelmed when he said he would be honored. "I would love to start a bible study group with you and Meg." What joy filled my heart when he said, "yes."

Little did I know that Lawrence, would become not only like a brother to me, but a fellow companion of our Savior and Shepherd in life, Jesus.

God gives us the choice to decide yes or no. "No" to remain silent, to do nothing, and to move on to worldly matters or we can respond, "Yes Lord, I will follow and trust in you." I myself in my early years, like most people, did not prepare for the afterlife, having been bogged down with the daily life of the world's affairs, a life confused by the constant cacophony of voices from the time we arise each day, calling to us to do this and do that. We prepare for school, vacations, retirement and every other type of earthly event, but do we nurture our soul for life forever after?

There are those who do not believe in an afterlife, who say, "We will find out some day sooner or later, hopefully later." At least those that do believe have something to look forward to. My trepidation-filled decision to ask Lawrence to be my partner in group bible study was the beginning of a long-time journey in Christ that would continue through many ensuing years, and even to this day. I was not aware of any consideration of my afterlife when I asked Lawrence that question, but this group would time and again place me in the position of answering God's call, forcing me to make decisions to say yes to a multitude of people in need. God would again place people in my life for me to help, even inviting me to courageously say yes, when my heart and mind knew it easier to just say no.

Wow! The dream I had for so long when walking out of my first bible study with Pat's friends on that Friday night was finally coming to fruition. Lawrence, Meg and I asked, "Where do we begin?"

We conferred with my spiritual director Fr. Michael, who said, "Pick a date for the first meeting, name the group, develop a format for the meeting, and then invite the church members to attend. No Problem!" Fr. Michael made it sound like a piece-of-cake. We decided to meet for an hour and a half, every Friday night to study the upcoming Sunday Mass scripture readings.

So, in the fall of 1995, Meg, Lawrence Chukwu, my close friends Don Warzhoka and Barbara Mankhen, Marcel Petriw and I met for our very first "*One Bread*

One Body" (OBOB) Sunday scripture study meeting. We named it based on the thought that we are all brothers and sisters in this One Body in Christ, and that our love is one with each other and with God. Our first weekly Friday evening meeting went without any hitches.

We started by inviting Jesus, the light of the world by lighting a candle representing His presence amidst us. We sang a song of praise, with lousy voices, but safety in numbers as they say. We began with the New Testament readings and then shared however our hearts were stirred or how God spoke to our hearts during the reading. This was followed by the Old Testament reading a Psalm and the Gospel reading, again sharing how the scripture moved our hearts, often applying the scripture to our everyday lives. We then read any commentaries available, either in the bible or another Catholic publication, which serves as affirmation to our interpretations, as everyone was asked to share. We concluded with prayers and petitions in thanking the Lord for all we have; we asked the Lord for forgiveness, mercy, healing, and transformation by filling our hearts with His love, and finally asked the Lord to send us out into the world to be His Light, Hope and Love, especially to the poor, sick, dying and lost. Lastly, a member blew out the candle. We finished with a song, shared any announcements, and ended by passing a jar to raise money for the needy. We collectively decide each year what organization will receive our donation.

The saying, "Be careful what you pray for; it may come true," refers to an unexpected twist leading to an unexpected calamity. In the case of OBOB, we got exactly what we prayed for and more. We experienced the many joys of growth in friendship, relationships, and our ministry over the years. As the weeks, months and years passed, our group grew to about twenty people, and we grew in the knowledge and love of the Lord and each other. Everyone that was prompted by the Holy Spirit to reach out to others inside and outside of our group and our missionary donations grew. Many lives have been affected by our group; the trickle continues to this day. As I look back, many of our outreach and charities were a reflection of the 12th step of A.A. I began to realize the incredible calling my Savior was asking of me.

No sooner had we started the group, than we were asked by Fr. Michael and Fr. Charlie to raise some money for a missionary priest in Nicaragua, their friend Fr. Doogan. He had a ministry in a small mountain village located in a dense forest, a hard journey from the city that often took over two months on horseback, bringing food and supplies in a wagon that often got stuck in the mud in the mountainous terrain. Fr. Doogan trod the journey to bring essentials and to hold Mass for the 200 villagers, and for most, he was the only priest they would see for the year. One Bread One Body group decided to take on the mission of raising money for Fr. Doogan as our first fundraiser. The mountain villagers are extremely poor, and largely dependent on Fr. Doogan's missionary work, and he in turn, relies solely on donations. We created a "Dollars for Doogan" jar placed on our table every week. It wasn't long before our first check was sent to him. Fr. Doogan is one of many missionaries we supported and continue to support.

This and the following stories illustrate of how someone reached out and touched our lives and, in that instant, either began or added to our recovery. We must have the unquestioning faith that our Savior will come to our aid and transform us from hopeless souls in darkness to instruments of His Light and Hope for others that still suffer. You may see yourself as those afflicted, but I assure you if you have the courage to take the first step in recovery, you will one day be the one living in the light and touching those still mired in the hopelessness of their darkness.

One of the many gifts of turning my life over to the care of my Savior was turning my attention from self to others, and thereby growing out of self-centeredness to caring and loving others. During my alcoholic years, I was consumed with satisfying my own needs instead of the needs of others. Thinking of others can be overwhelming but God has a way of presenting opportunities to us everywhere each and every day if we look for and take advantage of them. Foreign missionary work is not the only opportunity we have to minister to people in need. We can do it right-at work, at home, anywhere we go. This is not to say that during my binge years, I did not at times care for others, especially my family, but my decisions were egocentrically about me first, then others. With help, I learned that the essence of serving God is to serve others. In recovery, I began by taking baby steps in the right direction, propelled by my faith.

On one occasion, a couple in our OBOB scripture group, Bob and Cheryl Nettles, along with Meg and I were in a coffee shop when another new member named Kathy Gdula approached us. Kathy and her friend asked in desperation for our help in aiding a young single mother in her early thirties with four children. This young mother had been diagnosed with Stage-4 cancer, had very little money, and was living in an apartment without any furniture except for one mattress where mother and all four children slept together. Kathy asked if our (OBOB) group could help the young, newly diagnosed, cancer patient in some way. Moved by the sad story and by Kathy's fervent urging, the four of us emptied our pockets and agreed instantly that we would ask the scripture group for help. At the next meeting, the group agreed to help the young dying mother.

The group's acclamation in saying yes proved to be fruitful for all of us as it brought us closer together. We all rallied as a group and within a few days, the young woman was picking out furniture with us at a local Christian sharing center thrift store. We also provided her a full month's worth of food for her and the children and assisted delivering all the furniture and food to the barren apartment. We then agreed to help her until we were able to see her and her children faring well. This close-to-home experience with Kathy taught me that there are needy people amongst us every day that we do not even recognize unless we open our hearts to others. The beauty of watching Kathy totally dedicate and sacrifice herself for the sake of another also taught me to give more of myself. I experienced first-hand that it is so much more rewarding to give than to receive.

This was my first experience with time, talent, money and labor for the poor amongst us that all began with the courage of Kathy's invitation to help someone in need. Indeed, the underlying message here is that Kathy had to respond yes or no to the prompting within her heart, of God asking her to approach us for help. Kathy's courage and yes to God, rather than easily saying no and moving on was the difference. Kathy was another example of God placing people in our path and inviting us to share His unconditional love with them.

On another occasion, I took my four grown children to their ancestral home in beautiful Ireland. I had been there a few times before with Meg visiting her ancestral home sights, but this time I was experiencing great joy with my own children, witnessing and realizing their love for one another, as well as for me. Soon after arriving in Ireland, I realized my children had the gift of loving and serving others less fortunate than themselves. While attending Mass one day in Ireland, we noticed a young man sitting by himself, and as the church emptied, he stayed behind. Upon closer examination, we noticed his quivering and figured that his physical handicap was probably Multiple Sclerosis (MS). Without hesitation my children Billy, Stephen, Shawn and Mary approached the young man befriended him. He looked to be in his early thirties, and as we sat with him over the next several hours, we traded stories with him. As we left the dimming church, we wished him God's speed. This was yet another lesson in how reaching out to a stranger can be rewarding and enlightening, and again reinforced that it is better to give than to receive. Our trip came to an end, and the four children travel back to the United States without me. I stayed behind to meet Fr. Michael my spiritual director, on holiday from his Parish duties back in the States to revisit his hometown of Letterkenny, County Donegal. We had been planning this two-week golf trip to Ireland for some time, and Fr. Michael was really looking forward to it. We were also going to be guests at a concert put on by Fr. Michael's close friend Daniel O'Donnell, an internationally known Irish recording star and philanthropist. The stage was set for a grand two weeks of good Irish craic (fun).

I had only been in Ireland a few days with Fr. Michael when I once again had an experience that would impact me forever. Fr. Michael and I were scheduled to play golf the next week with Daniel, and stay there on the Northwest Coast of Ireland, in Daniel's hometown of Kinkasslagh, County Donegal. On the morning we were to meet up with Daniel, the day of his annual concert for charity where people came by the thousands from everywhere, Fr. Michael explained that he himself was not going to attend the concert, nor be able to stay for the week of golf. I looked at him astonished, knowing how he had been anticipating these two fun weeks. I instantly thought he was jesting. But no, our fun and gold-at-the-end-of-the-rainbow golf game day had been interrupted by a phone call informing him that a priest he had not seen in twenty years had just been convicted of pedophilia at the age of seventy-one and imprisoned for eleven years.

Fr. Michael felt compelled to visit his old friend in prison to minister and console this aged priest now ostracized from most all of society. I was so stunned in part because I knew he had been looking forward so much to this week of fun and relaxation. I also was in incredible awe at the love he had for his fellow priest that it transcended all emotions; clearly, his love from within his heart to serve others was absolute. I questioned his decision and asked, "Why couldn't you just pray for this priest?" I questioned him especially since he had not spoken or seen him for twenty years, and in this way, he could still enjoy himself and continue on his planned vacation.

Fr. Michael's love for his fellow brother priest and friend from the past reached beyond his own peace and joy; Fr. Michael's love was to bring peace and joy to his fallen friend instead. I knew I wanted to possess that radical love, and without hesitation, told him I would accompany him on the 8-hour trip to the prison, foregoing the concert and golf; I wanted to be by Fr. Michael's side as a friend and to experience first-hand his ministry to a prisoner and fellow friend in hopes that I too could bring this peace and joy to others. Unfortunately, I had to wait outside the prison for three to four hours while Fr. Michael ministered to his friend. What a lesson of giving rather than receiving to the imprisoned priest, a bringing of hope to the broken—a clear lesson of hating the sin and loving the sinner.

PART FOUR

Becoming the Word

Chapter 14

Where You Cannot Find Love
Put Love — Then You Will Find Love

FROM OUR HUMAN vantage point, it is quite easy to not only hate the despicable, sinful nature of the pedophile but to also despise and hate the pedophile as well. However, if we recall in scripture, Jesus tells His disciples, "We must love our enemies." What a command, which is so much against our human nature. So how can we hate the sin but love the sinner? There are probably many times that we think it impossible, but there is nothing impossible with God. When we think there is no way, God finds a way. It is only through the grace of God that we can at the same time love the sinner, but hate the sin, whose often egregious sinfulness not only gravely offends ourselves but God as well. We must find a way to eradicate those hateful feelings, less we jeopardize salvation.

Let us not forget Jesus telling His disciples, "At the end of each of our lives we will be judged on how we loved others, especially the least of our brothers," hence, we also will be judged on how we judged others. If we condemn others, we risk the same condemnation upon ourselves. Receiving forgiveness for ourselves thru personal reconciliation or confession and working A.A. Steps 4, 5 and 6 allows us to in turn forgive others, thus transforming us into the light of our Savior. We should cry out to Our Savior for the grace to love like Him unconditionally, for it is through love that we will gain eternal life with the Lord.

It has been said we can miss out on heaven by 18 inches- the length between our brain and our heart. We must not only nourish our brain with the Word of our Savior, but our heart as well. There must be a migration of this knowledge from the brain to the heart and back. This will allow us to conform to our Savior's will, but with sincerity of heart. Too often we seek our Savior's will outside of us instead of within us. Once we have knowledge of our Savior's will through an informed conscience, we can more readily answer life's challenges. Many times, we are conflicted between what the world is saying, or what our Savior is saying. We are confronted with this question: Do we have duplicity of heart? We know what the Spirit is speaking to us, but succumb to the world's beguiling ways.

One of the greatest blessings I've received in my years of recovery has been the opportunity to journey to Third World countries and work with the disenfranchised and marginalized whose unspeakable suffering, living conditions, and political injustices cause an aberration within our minds, hearts and deep down in our souls. Our hearts and minds cry out, "How can these conditions be so unfair, so unjust?"

On one such journey to rural Nigeria, we were stunned at the sight of dead bodies along the roadside, garbage piled head high in the medians due to lack of government support, people dying decades prematurely of common diseases due to lack of medications. Massive government corruption and the increasingly ever-present encroachment by the terrorist group Boka Haram contributed to the plight of the local people. The ability and opportunities I have had to extend my migration from brain to heart, down to my feet and back again, undoubtedly contributed to me coming full circle to create my desire to make a difference in the world. I am unequivocally sure these experiences helped shape and define my future desires and aspirations for serving mankind. "He who returns from a journey is not the same as he who left." But it is only possible through the transforming grace and knowledge of our Savior, as we reason in our sober state of mind.

I feel that this transformation for me was wrought from four mini-miraculous moments. First, the moment I totally surrendered myself to the care of my Savior. We must be resolute in our commitment in turning our will and our life over to the care of our Savior. Half-hearted measures will prove to be fruitless and to no avail. Second, the moment when through confession and working A.A. Steps 4 to 7, I emptied all the baggage, suffering, anguish of my soul and readied myself to be cleansed of all the torment.

A major roadblock for most addicts occurs during this step. However, if you are disinclined to confess or share your sinfulness face-to-face, refusing to expose your dark side or perhaps fearful of exposing your past ignominious behavior, put your mind to rest. Your confessor, whether your sponsor or priest or whomever, is bound by oath to hear your confession with total confidentiality and anonymity.

The third transforming miraculous event, besides surrendering to God and reconciling my sins and transgressions, that took place in my personal recovery and returned to sanity and inner peace, occurred while consuming the Eucharist of our Savior. However, I would like to preface the upcoming story regarding this, by stating that this is not embodied in A.A.'s program or steps to recovery, nor is it essential in your own personal recovery. I am simply stating that the Eucharist brought a miraculous change of heart, mind and soul not only to me, but to two other addicts we will soon hear about, both interestingly enough non-Catholics. So, let's continue with an open mind.

By receiving the Eucharist of our Savior, I felt transformed into His love, the love that brings "new life" and gives us peace and hope. After receiving our Savior through the Holy Eucharist, we become a conduit of His Love challenging us to go out into the world, becoming His love to others. We go forth into the world to bring forgiveness, healing and transformation through love by reaching out to others, broken in some form, as we too are people broken in some way. It was a moving experience for me, and it helped shape my heart and mind, so when the opportunity to reach out arose, it helped ready me to accept the challenge to say "Yes."

We feed ourselves on both the Spirit and Eucharist of our Savior, not only for our own sanctification and redemption, but to go out into the world so it may in a sense feed on us. Explanation of this can be found in the Gospels of Mark, Luke, Matthew as well as the gospel of John and in the Acts of the Apostles. Simply put, the intent and hope one has in receiving the Eucharist is to be transformed into our Savior's love, the love that our Savior says, "Brings new life," and gives one peace and hope of living eternally with Him. Once again, my explaining the Eucharist is not an attempt to sway you or draw you into the Catholic Church. It is merely conveying my experience, belief and the perceived miraculous change and transformation it had on my mind, heart and soul and catapulted my recovery to the fourth miraculous event, intensifying my thirst and hunger to, through scripture, learn everything there is to know about my Savior.

This next story illustrates how the Eucharist effected a miraculous change on two non-Catholics. It begins on a Friday night at our OBOB bible study of the Sunday Scripture readings. When the meeting ended, a Jamaican woman named Pam, who converted from Jehovah Witness to Catholicism, approached me asking for a favor. Pam was a fervent follower of Jesus with eyes always looking out for the welfare of others; she always put others first above herself. She was terribly upset this particular Friday evening, explaining that her nephew, Delroy, now in his mid-forties, whom she had not seen in 20 years, called the night before. She had gone immediately to pick him up at the local bus station. Pam had found him disheveled, deathly sick, filthy dirty, and smelling horribly. Delroy had proceeded to tell Pam that he had full-blown AIDS. His family had totally ostracized him, virtually disowned him, and left him homeless. She was at a loss for words and did not know how to comfort or tend to him.

I agreed to meet Delroy, and we immediately cared for him and were able to place him in a temporary shelter exclusively for HIV/AIDS afflicted people. Once he settled in, I asked Delroy if he would like to have a weekly bible study with some fellow AIDS victims. Although he was not religious, he agreed thankfully. We embraced and as our tears met, I felt the emptiness of his despair begin to fill ever so slightly with a glimmer of hope, love and dignity.

At that moment I recalled years back at a meeting with a panel of AIDS victims, when Fr. Michael Cannon had stood up and rebuked the theory that God would condemn these victims, and instead maintained He would embrace them. From then on, we held bible studies for the critically ill AIDS victims at the facility, singing, studying scripture and praying. I emphasized to these physically suffering people that we all share one thing in common-the love we each have for one another that can transcend all divisiveness, bigotry and hatred that may exist within us. We are all one in Christ Jesus who died for us so that we may have eternal life. Although our plights and junctures in the paths of life may differ, our love amongst each other is one in Christ our Savior.

Soon thereafter, these scripture meetings turned into something more.

My Irish priest and friend Fr. Joe Young agreed to hold Mass and confessions after our bible studies. Our group was astonished when Delroy, after confessing his sins and receiving the Eucharist, was transformed from despair to hope, darkness to light, self-deprecation to loving himself. Delroy, who had become our friend, eventually died of AIDS within six months, but passed knowing he was loved by us and by God and died with dignity.

On another occasion with our scripture study about to begin, a woman in her mid-thirties walked in with her six-year-old daughter. Her name was Esther, and she was homeless, and ill with full-blown AIDS. Two weeks prior she had been found, in a gutter near death from an overdose, and lacking any hope in a life that she wanted to end. She was consumed with self-deprecation, shame, guilt, despair, and totally hating life. While attending Mass with Fr. Joe, I could not help but pity Esther, because, though she was physically in the room, she was mentally not there with us. Her heart was so hardened, and the doors to her heart were so completely shut with pain that she was unable to receive our love or the love from God and had become embittered by life. Her daughter's well-being remained her sole motive in holding on. For whatever reason, she continued to come back every week in silence, still angry and still hopeless.

Then one evening weeks later, she became willing to let God into her heart. She sat with Father Joe confessing her transgressions, emptying her burdens in total surrender, willing to receive God's forgiveness. As she received the Eucharist from Fr. Joe, I witnessed a glow on her face, the miracle of transforming into God's love, a look as if she were evolving into a beautiful rose, opening up to God and learning to trust others. She became joyfully elated over time as she went from the depth of darkness and despair into the light of hope and love. She went from Serpent to Savior; and she went from total hopelessness to hope, that is, to searching for ways of a better life for herself and her daughter and becoming a light for countless others lost in the darkness of sin. I witnessed Esther's transformation from receiving the Eucharist, as I had Delroy's, from being blinded by tears of sadness and despair to facial expressions of joy and hope.

One Bread One Body was able to help her financially including housing her and her daughter along with Delroy and two other aids victims, thanks to the generosity of a friend Mary D. who purchased the house, with the provision that our scripture group would manage it for her. Ten years later, Esther had her own little business of knitting and crocheting, a trade learned from her grandmother. She began selling her handmade wares online and had earned enough money to live a modest life and send her daughter to and graduate from Veterinarian School. What a lesson learned by all of us for extending compassionate love and patience to a distressed mother.

Both Esther's and Delroy's transformation reminded me of a poem read by my mentor Monsignor Patrick Caverly, my first confessor after my returning back to church after 25 years. The poem is called "The Touch of the Master's Hand."

'Twas battered and scarred. And the auctioneer
　　Thought it scarcely worth his while
　　To waste much time on the old violin,
　　But held it up with a smile.

"What am I bid good folks," he cried,
　　"Who'll start the bidding for me?
　　A dollar, a dollar, Then two! Only two?
　　Two dollars, and who'll make it three?"

"Three dollars once, three dollars, twice;
　　Going for three —" But no,
　　From the room, far back, a grey-haired man
　　Came forward and picked up the bow;

Then wiping the dust from the old violin,
　　And tightening the loosened strings,
　　He played a melody pure and sweet,

As a caroling angel sings.

The music ceased, and the auctioneer,
*   With a voice that was quiet and low,*
*   Said: "What am I bid for the old violin?"*
*   And he held it up with the bow.*

"A thousand dollars, and who'll make it two?
*   Two thousand! And who'll make it three.*
*   Three thousand, once; three thousand twice,*
*   And going and gone," said he.*

The people cheered, but some of them cried,
*   "We do not quite understand.*
*   What changed its worth?" Swift came the*
*   reply: "The touch of the Master's hand."*

And many a man with life out of tune,
*   And battered and scarred with sin,*
*   Is auctioned cheap to the thoughtless crowd*
*   Much like the old violin.*

A "Mess of pottage, a glass of wine,"
*   A game—and he travels on.*
*   He is "Going" once, and "Going" twice,*

He's "Going" and almost "Gone."

But the Master comes, and the foolish crowd
  Never can quite understand
  The worth of a soul and the change that is
  wrought
  By the touch of the Masters hand.

WE ALL LEARNED that God could and would restore us to sanity if we sought Him; He can and will heal and restore our lives if we let Him into our lives, by having the faith and courage to cry-out, asking for His help. Another lesson learned here is that in each case, my own, Delroy's, and Esther's, someone reached out to us with an invitation. An invitation in hopes that they too might experience the touch of the Master's hand. So, let us not forget that we have the power of God within us and are able to reach out to those who still suffer.

Chapter 15

They Will Know You Are My Disciples by Your Love

OUR OBOB OUTREACHES started out small, but gradually became larger as our confidence grew. I will include some examples of smaller projects here simply to show one does not have to have a host of skills and talents to reach out to others. Endless numbers of individuals exist in the world who are desperately in need. I was amazed myself at how experiencing the smallest outreach to a single soul can lift your spirits and supply a whole new interest in life. It can be a powerful engine to turn from addiction, but only if the ground is prepared by the steps that allow letting go of total self-interest. Note in these stories that I will often be using "our" instead of "I." This is no accident. I was becoming immersed in this new perspective. Forming the scripture study group was much more important than I realized at the time. Outreach does not need others traveling the same road, but it certainly helps. Note also that fund raising becomes an important component of larger projects but can supply the same spiritual lift.

The first story started with a voice from the back of the room. It illustrates the power of one, and how one person can truly make a difference in the lives of others. Each year in a OBOB meeting during the Lenten season, the group picks an outreach for Lent and the group raises money for that project. Sal in the back of the room, a single voice, suggested that we help the hundreds of homeless that live locally in the woods. Another member chimed in "In addition to bringing food, water and supplies, it will give them hope as well." This was enough to inspire another person to chime in and suggest "Let it be called Bags of Hope." Mark and Rhonda spontaneously decided to form an outreach calling it Bags of Hope, a reality that would in the months and years following, up to this very day, feed and clothe thousands of men, women and children, destitute, sick, hungry and homeless. Rhonda said that "We will begin this outreach with total trust in God."

On one occasion Mark, Rhonda and I were bringing Bags of Hope into a mosquito infested woods where the authorities told us hundreds of people living. Once in the woods we ran into a woman named Doris, in her mid-40s along with two elderly men. It was evident she was homeless and had lived in the woods for a long time. Her skin black with dirt, she was gaunt and disheveled, her eyes revealed her sadness and hopelessness. Having been out into the rainy woods all day I personally was aghast and moved at her appearance but totally clueless as how to immediately help her. I was physically spent and anxious to leave. But no. Rhonda stopped suddenly, turned around and approached the woman, then instructed me to get water and a towel. She took the towel and the water and gently washed the woman's arms and face and as the dirt slowly disappeared, tears blinded all of us present.

It was a lesson that I would learn firsthand. Often times we are confronted with chances to reach out to those lost, broken, but for whatever the reason we find it easier to dismiss the thought of helping and move on to another thought. I realized watching Rhonda that it is in those times when everything is telling us "No, just move on," we should say, "yes, Lord give me the strength to get involved."

On our way out of the woods that day driving home, Rhonda, again thinking not about herself, but about those less fortunate, said, "Let's put her up in a hotel for a week, with enough food to last her." I did not realize it then, but months later reflecting back on this incident it reminded me of the Scripture reading in the Gospel of Luke in the New Testament about the good Samaritan:

Luke Writes: Just then a lawyer stood up to test Jesus. "Teacher," he said, "What must I do to inherit eternal life?" Jesus said to him, "What is written in the law? What do you read there?" He answered, "You shall love the Lord your God with all your heart, and with all your soul, and with all your strength, and with all your mind; and your neighbor as yourself." And he said to him, "You have given the right answer; do this, and you will live."

But wanting to justify himself, he asked Jesus, "And who is my neighbor?" Jesus replied, "A man was going down from Jerusalem to Jericho, and fell into the hands of robbers, who stripped him, beat him, and went away, leaving him half dead. Now by chance a priest was going down that road; and when he saw him, he passed by on the other side. So likewise, a Levite, when he came to the place and saw him, passed by on the other side. But a Samaritan while traveling came near him; and when he saw him, he was moved with pity. He went to him and bandaged his wounds, having poured oil and wine on them. Then he put him on his own animal, brought him to an inn, and took care of him. The next day he took out two denarii, gave them to the innkeeper and said, 'Take care of him; and when I come back, I will repay you what ever more you spend.' " "Which of these three, do you think, was a neighbor to the man who fell into the hands of the robbers?" Jesus said. "The one who showed him mercy." Said the lawyer. Jesus replied, "Go and do likewise."

We turned the truck around and traveled back to the woods, gathered Doris, got her settled in a hotel room, and instructed the hotel to take care of her for a week, and if there was any other expense, we would absorb it. Mark and Rhonda eventually were able to place Doris into a safe haven community which helped her reconnect with some of her family up north, and subsequently made arrangements to move her there.

The Bags of Hope project continued feverishly. We spent much time with the local authorities who aided us in locating the pockets of homeless living in the woods all over central Florida. This enabled us in the following months to pass out over 3000 Bags of Hope weekly, each involving someone's personal story. One day, Rhonda told us one of these stories: that of Big John, a survivor in the woods for years. Rhonda was out in the woods visiting and bringing food and supplies to Big John. But as she approached his makeshift tent, she was stunned and shocked at the sight of him. As he lay prostrate in his defecation and urine, he sadly looked up at her unable to move. He called to her, "I'm extremely sick and I cannot move. I'm going to die here today Rhonda." Characteristically, Rhonda looked at him and replied: "You may die today Big John, but you will not die here." Then she put his arm around her shoulder and somehow got him to his feet and carried him to her truck and to the hospital.

When chronic homeless are treated in the hospital, the hospital typically treats them as best they can and then releases them back out into the streets. Consequently, hundreds of homeless are chronically ill as well. Mark and Rhonda, along with other OBOB members and volunteers, were able to get Big John, once he left the hospital, to a 90-day halfway house called Pathways to Care. It housed chronically ill homeless for 90 days, until they were able to find permanent residence for them.

It would also become one of OBOB's outreach ministries. In addition to financial help, each Christmas, in the Pathways community room, we would sing Christmas carols with the residents, bring them gifts, and share a meal. Those who were too ill to come to the community room were visited by caroling OBOB members bringing them their presents.

Big John stayed there for three months until Mark and Rhonda found a permanent residence for him to live out the rest of his life. Eventually, months later, he died of his cancer, but with dignity and knowing he was loved. Mark and Rhonda stayed in close contact with him right to the end and made arrangements for his funeral and burial. This story exemplifies what a fine example of one person's suggestion of reaching out and another person taking that notion and manifesting it into reality.

We never know whether our suggestions or our decisions to act in kindness and love towards the needy will at some future point effect a change for the better. Senator Robert F. Kennedy, brother of President John F. Kennedy once said in a speech in Cape Town S. Africa in the height of apartheid, "Few will have the greatness to bend history itself. But each of us can act to change a small portion of events. And in the confluence of all those acts will be written the history of this generation. Each time a man stands up for an ideal or acts to improve the lot of others or strikes out against injustice, he sends forth a tiny ripple of hope, and crossing each other from a million different centers of energy and daring, those ripples build a current that will sweep down the mightiest walls of oppression and resistance."

On another occasion I was passenger with Mark and Rhonda on the way to drop off Bags of Hope (though we had come to call them BOH) in the woods for the homeless. The truck was full of Bags of Hope and the day would be full distributing them to the several homeless locations throughout Central Florida. On the way to our first location, I think I witnessed what love looks like. Mark, driving down a busy road, cars buzzing to and fro, suddenly slammed on his brakes and pulled onto the sidewalk, abruptly coming to a complete stop. In an instant he opened the door, scurrying to the back of the truck to grab a BOH. Rhonda and I both asked him what happened. What are you doing? He exuberantly replied, "There's a homeless man across the street." Then Mark was gone, grinning from ear to ear, scampering across the busy road to meet the homeless man and give him a BOH. Later as I pondered that event, I concluded that Mark's heart sighting the homeless man, in a sense, exploded with pure unconditional love. His heart leapt with joy in hopes of meeting and sharing our Savior's love. I think that's one example of what love looks like.

Bags of Hope eventually expanded its outreach into helping hundreds and hundreds of poor migrant children by feeding, clothing and educating them. Each week ten or twenty Bags of Hope volunteers would act as Big Brother mentoring the children—taking them books and help them read and write. Bags of Hope continues to this day as a 501C3 Charitable Organization, catering to hundreds of homeless, destitute, wayward lost souls.

Again, I write these experiences, not to show you how many great things I have done but to convince you that God can and will take the worst and most despicable, as I was a lot of the time, and touch them with his healing hand, transform them and send them out into the world to spread His love. Each of these experiences I share with you are little miracles that happened in my life only because I made a little decision to say "Yes" God, I will try again to change my life. I am a sorrowful alcoholic, my life was totally unmanageable and only God could and would if I sought him out, allow me to change and take another path in life. I could continue chapter after chapter with these little miracle stories I've experienced but I will continue with just a few more that had a profound effect on me.

One afternoon I stopped at a convenience store for a cold drink. At the checkout counter was a big jar with a poster asking for donations. It read donations for these three young teen age girls whose mother was killed a few days prior in an auto accident. To make it worse their father had been killed a few years ago. Tragically now the girls were without both their mother and their father. My heart sinking, I deposited some money, gave the clerk my business card and told her if they needed help call me. You've heard it said. "Watch what you pray for." Well, it was not more than a few days later that I received a call from the girls' aunt. She said she did not have much money but chose to raise the children despite the fact she was close to retirement and probably would have to remain working. I asked her what was needed, and she said they virtually needed everything. She revealed to me she had very little income and didn't know how she was going to manage but was undeterred knowing God would find a way. The time of this tragedy was right before Christmas. Such an unbelievably sad situation.

Having heard the tragic story, I immediately shared it with our One Bread One Body Scripture study group. Without hesitation everyone chimed in "Let us do something." Within a few days we made a visit to meet the girls and their aunt. Entering the apartment, we were stunned to see how small it was, and wondered how four people could possibly live there with only two bedrooms and one small bath. We also noticed a little Christmas tree adorned with a few lights, with no gifts beneath it. We all left on a mission. We didn't know how or what we could do but knew if we said, "Yes," God would show us the way.

Bingo. Within a few days we'd gathered enough donations for Christmas gifts and groceries and received a phone call from our wealthy lady friend Mary D. She decided to make this her company's Christmas outreach raising thousands of dollars. One of her executives stated he was giving a lifelong monetary gift to the family. God does incredible things using each of us if we only surrender to him. Let go, let God. Where we think there is no way God makes a way.

Christmas Eve we visited the girls and their aunt, taking them the food and decorating the tree, leaving several presents for each of them. The girls were overwhelmed with tears, and we all embraced, sharing our love for one another. Thanks be to God our Savior; arrangements were eventually made for the girls to attend a local private Catholic school, and for the aunt and girls to move into a larger apartment.

My last little story occurred as I walked into a 7-11 convenience store. A woman clerk stopped me and asked if I wasn't Bill Mitchell from the Scripture outreach group One Bread One Body. I replied, 'I am he'.

"Would you and your group be able to help two young girls?" She asked. They were visiting their aunt here in Orlando from St. Louis and were hoping to go to Disney World. That night, a few hours after having arrived at their aunt's home, they went into her bedroom only to find their aunt dead. The girls, age 5 and 9, had no one to turn to. Their mother back in St. Louis was in dire money straits, heavily addicted, and just trying to get by day to day. The aunt that passed away, come to find out, had almost no money and none for a funeral or burial. The convenience clerk pleaded with me to see if we could somehow help. I soon got the word out to our OBOB group, and we raise funds to get the girls, and the deceased aunt, back to St. Louis, and to provide for a funeral and burial for the aunt. We also escorted the girls to Disney World before they left.

The story illustrates what can happen to those mired

in any form of addiction, but willing to take the steps to begin recovery. As we become sober, clean and stronger spiritually, our eyes through the Grace of God, turn away from ourselves and our selfishness to accepting the call to help others, either those who still suffer with addiction, or those who have fallen upon bad times. St. Francis of Assisi, a Catholic Franciscan monk in the 13th century, epitomizes this transformation of mind and heart. You may recognize the prayer that has long been associated with him:

Lord, make me an instrument of your peace,
where there is hatred, let me sow love,
where there is injury, pardon,
where there is doubt, faith,
where there is despair, hope,
where there is darkness, light,
where there is sadness, joy

O Devine Master, grant that I may not so much
seek to be consoled as to console,
to be understood as to understand,
to be loved as to love,
for it is in giving that we receive,
it is in pardoning that we are pardoned,
and it is in dying that we are born to eternal
life.   *Amen*

Chapter 16

Are We Our Brother's Keepers?

"One person can make a difference,

and everyone should try."

—President John F. Kennedy

THIS NEXT OUTREACH was in a foreign country, giving me great insight and clarity into sharing God's love outside the borders of my own country. In the previous chapter we read what Jesus taught about who is our neighbor. Are there borders to Gods' Love? Franciscan priest Fr.

Patrick Quinn once exclaimed, "Are we Americans who happened to be Christians, or are we Christians who happened to be Americans?" It's a great quote to ponder and meditate on. It recalls the challenging question, "Are we our brothers' keepers? Are there any borders to God's love? If we genuinely believe we are God's children and followers of our Lord and Savior, are we called to reach out beyond our borders to strangers and foreigners?"

One of our OBOB members, previously introduced, Jamaican Pam, invited me to such a challenge. This foreign outreach was working with the Missionaries of the Poor, a Catholic order of priests and brothers. Their home mission was located in Pam's hometown, Kingston, Jamaica, an extremely impoverished city full of graft and crime. The order was founded by a Chinese Jamaican named Father Richard Ho Lung. For many years he was a professor at Boston College, but deep down inside felt his calling was to tend to the needy, forgotten, helpless, and homeless in the ghettos of his birthplace, Kingston. He obtained approval from the Pope in Rome to start a new order to be named The Missionaries of the Poor, who would take in, and in a sense, adopt all those who could not survive on their own, and whose relatives were too poor to support and tend to them. From babies born with defects, to the elderly unable to take care for themselves, to the mentally challenged, the physically handicapped, those suffering from deadly disease such as AIDS, and many, many more, these unfortunates were welcomed and ministered to by the MOPs (as the missionaries came to be called).

Each morning, noon and night the MOP brothers would drive to their three compounds where some 400 resident patients were housed, fed, cleaned, and medicated. The Brothers shared God's word and love until their final day on this earth. This was their vocation seven days a week. Throughout the year they would invite people worldwide to join them and help out in the compounds. In response, people would come from all parts of the world to share God's love with the 400 residents and help out.

Soon after my assent to travel to the Kingston mission, Pam and I and a few other OBOB members arrived in Jamaica and were put up in a small compound by the MOP brothers. After early breakfast, Mass and orientation with the MOP's, we were driven to the compound housing the 400+ residents. In the van with the Brothers as we pulled up to the gate that opened to one of the compounds, I was profoundly moved by the sight of three remarkable residents on their way to lunch. One man with no legs was in a wheelchair; he was being pushed in the wheelchair by a young man who had Down Syndrome; behind him, grasping his shoulder, was a blind man. At that moment I realized that no matter what our circumstances in life, we are called to tend to each other when in need. After spending the week there, I knew I was destined to someday return.

Upon my arrival back in the States, I couldn't wait to share my experiences with Meg, my family, and the scripture outreach, OBOB. It was during the time of year Meg's kindergarten class would have a bake sale and donate the money to a charity of their choice. With the parents baking the cookies and cakes, the children, dressed in their bakers' hats, sold all the bake goods, raising over a thousand dollars to be sent to the MOPs as their charity of choice. Another great lesson learned.

As we recall in an earlier chapter Robert F. Kennedy once said, "Each good deed, each time we give of ourselves for the betterment of mankind creates a ripple of hope that in time can affect change for the good." In my case, this ripple effect started by someone inviting me to participate in reaching out to the needy; my saying, "yes" to the invitation leading to my experiencing this outreach, to sharing this experience with others, and finally, this story being passed down to children, who together exuberantly reach out as young five and six-year-olds to help the MOPs as their chosen mission. My heart yearned to one day return. OBOB continued to raise money over the years and send it to Kingston. And so, the ripples were there.

Some years later I asked one of my daughters, Shawn, a nurse practitioner, if she would like to join me on this next mission trip. She emphatically said, "Of course!" And so, our plans were set. Unfortunately, when the time came to board our plane to Kingston, a massive hurricane was fast approaching Jamaica. After weighing the possible danger involved, and after conferring with husband John, Shawn decided to forgo the mission trip, because their four children were still barely in their teens, and she didn't want to chance it. I was going to go, no matter what, knowing the MOPs would need even more help if the hurricane hit. When Shawn called the night before my departure, and told me of her decision, I was of course terribly disappointed, but totally understood. She did however insist on driving me to the airport the next morning.

Morning came, and on the way, she asked if I was nervous about going, and I replied, "Not really." I was going on God's mission to share His love and was confident he would protect and shield me. After a few minutes of silence Shawn looked at me and said, "Dad, I'm going with you. My suitcase is still in the trunk of the car all packed. I'm getting a strong message in my heart that this is what God wants me to do." She called her husband John, got his blessing and the rest is history as they say. We were soon on the plane, and landing in Kingston. The MOP's greeted us and drove us to our accommodations. The weekend was full of spiritual gifts. We soon found that by helping the less fortunate, we ended up receiving much, much more than what we were giving.

Three experiences at the compounds stood out amongst the many. On one occasion I noticed a little four-year-old boy named Johnny sitting on the steps, one arm grasping the rail, head down, his face an image of emptiness and sadness. I sat down next to him putting my arm around him. There was nothing I could say. They told me his mom had just died of AIDS.

As we sat there, I soon realized he was in a total helplessly saddened state unable to give love or receive love. After several minutes he finally rested his head on my shoulder. We sat there in silence. My heart was broken knowing this episode of exchanging our love would be soon gone. I later learned that little Johnny, like his mother, had died of AIDS.

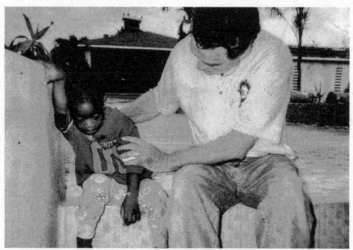

Figure 1. Heart wrenching picture of little Johnny's grief and sense of loss following his mother's death from AIDS.

HIS EMPTINESS REPRESENTS the great famine of love in the world and our call to reach out.

Another experience at the compound came working with MOP's Fr. Matthew. He asked if I would help him in the AIDS unit. Having had experience working with AIDS victims in our One Bread One Body outreach group, I accepted. Fr. Matthew related to me that when he came from India to join the MOP's he told them he would do anything, but he could not work in the AIDS unit. He just wasn't cut out for that. But he went on to say that this day marked 11 years that he had been here, working in the AIDS unit. "Every morning now when I arise, I cannot wait to get here to be with my brothers afflicted with this condition. God changes us and transforms us. We merely have to respond to him by saying yes."

Probably the most touching experience came when my daughter Shawn approached me after I had finished helping out with Fr. Matthew. She said she was working with the elderly, and one resident, Ms. Foster, in her 90s was near death. I asked Shawn if I could help. She responded by telling me it would be extremely hard to see Ms. Foster in the state that she was in, and I'd better not. I replied, "Yes, but I will help you anyway, Shawn." After putting on my facial mask and gloves and smock, I entered into the room where Ms. Foster lay. I was utterly shocked. Poor Ms. Foster was lying there on a vinyl rubber mat, no pillow, with open gaping sores filled with maggots, and flies all around. I felt helpless as I watched Shawn gently clean each gaping sore, each time listening to the terrible moan of pain from Ms. Foster. Feeling helpless, I could only caress her head and softly sing in her ears a beautiful song, "Be with me Lord. Be with me Lord. When I'm in trouble and I don't know where to go. Be with me Lord." Over and over, I sang, as Shawn tried as gently as possible to clean all the sores, tears flowing from Shawn's eyes. Suddenly, ever so softly, I could hear Ms. Foster, barely able to muster words because of the indescribable pain: "Be with me Lord."

We finally cleaned Ms. Foster, put a clean new cotton robe on her, and laid her back down on the rubber cot, again with not even a pillow to rest her head. The MOPs are totally self-supporting, surviving only on donations. They grow their own food, have only two robes each to wear. One pair of sandals, living only to share God's love with the ones no one wants to care for, each day and every day. After praying with Ms. Foster, we left the compound. I said to Shawn that we must go find a pillow for Ms. Foster and get her some beautiful smelling flowers to rest next to her head so she can smell them. Shawn said that while she was tending to Ms. Foster, she prayed that God would take her home soon. Ms. Foster was never married and had outlived all relatives. She lay there in excruciating pain alone. We left that afternoon on a mission: to find a pillow and to gather the most beautiful, scent-filled flowers in Kingston. Finally, as the day came to an end, we had gathered both the pillow and the flowers. We couldn't wait for the next morning to visit Ms. Foster.

Morning came. 7 AM Mass with the MOP's, breakfast, and then on our way to the compound to visit Ms. Foster. Entering the compound, we anxiously walked to Ms. Foster's room. We opened the door and were stunned finding her body covered with a sheet. A MOP brother said to us that she died last night, peacefully. We gently lifted her head and rested it on the pillow and placed the beautiful flowers upon her, thanking God for taking her home. We relayed the story to our friend Pam, who accompanied us on the mission trip, and Pam remarked, "Both you and Shawn last night dressed her wounds, but more importantly cleaned her, preparing her to meet the Lord."

Our weekend ended the next day, celebrating Mass with all the residents, and thanking God for allowing us to be privileged to meet them all. The relationship between OBOB and MOP grew, and when possible, we helped them financially as much as we could. On one occasion, I received an email from a MOP, Fr. Raymond, imploring me and the OBOB group, if possible, raise money for a dire need in remote India where he was ministering. There was a colony of leprosy-afflicted children that he was taking care of in their little hamlet.

The well from which they draw their potable water had become polluted and was drying up. A new well had to be drilled quickly. Fr. Raymond's frantic plea was to get the well dug immediately, because they were getting deathly sick from drinking the contaminated water from the well. My response was like all the rest of the pleas I received over the years: I reached out to my fellow OBOB members. Somehow, within just a few days after we sent out an email to all the members, OBOB miraculously raised the thousands of dollars needed to dig a new well.

Again, I write about these experiences, not to show you how many great things I've done, but to convince you that God can and will take the worst and most despicable, as I had been a lot of the time, and touch us with His healing hand, transform us, and send us out into the world to spread His Love. Each of those experiences I share with you are little miracles that happened in my life only because I made a little decision to say, "Yes, I will try again to change my life. I am a sorrowful alcoholic, my life was totally unmanageable, and only God could and would, if I sought him out, allow me to change, and take another path in life."

All of our future outreach projects both locally and internationally are too many to mention, but I want to relate enough to convey the point that in ministries, size does not matter. Helping a sick homeless beggar on the street may even require more compassion than fund raising for a large project. Both are work that cries out to be done. The quote of Christ Jesus is apt here: "There is no greater love than to give up one's life for another." The MOPs, for example, have certainly done this, but they have done more, because they involved others all over the world.

A personal example of this was when our OBOB group raised money for the MOP's and when Meg's kindergarten class at the academy had a bake sale raising $1000's for them as well. We continued to contribute to Missionaries of the Poor, and over several years some eventually traveled to Kingston on mission trips, helping along with the MOP's the marginalized and forgotten. Our stories of outreach are shared to assure others still struggling with addiction, depression, fear, guilt, shame, and even those with fairly comfortable lives, that anything is possible with the help of God.

It is not at all so important in life in what we attain, whether it is power, prestige or wealth. It is far more important in life in what we give to others, especially the least of our brothers. We live in a society where we are judged on how far up the ladder we climb and how many possessions we have amassed. While we do not condemn or judge these heights that some have attained in life, for we are called to do the best we can with the God given talents we possess, it is more important we become the best person that God has called us to become, using the gifts He has given us at birth, to be children of God with Heaven as our goal, attaining eternal life with Him. Unless we keep our eyes and ears alerted to those in need by giving and caring for others, we risk having our successes becoming curses at the end of our life rather than blessings. As the saying goes, "It's nice to be important but it is more important to be nice."

So too, with those of us who have given up our addictions, our sinful life, we are called in the same way to affix our minds, hearts, eyes, and ears to those crying out or suffering, or living in some form of darkness; we are called to help others as Jesus came to help not the rich but the sinner. When we rise above and look beyond our plight in life and take the steps to march out of the darkness of addiction into the light of new life, we can then become instruments of peace, hope and love for others.

In the concluding chapters, I will share the simple steps to attain the true meaning of life, the life that God created in each and every one of us, in His likeness and image, to follow the Gospel message taught to us by Jesus. There is limited happiness in following the ways of the world, for something seems always to be missing deep down inside of us, and that something is the connection to the spiritual world.

Chapter 17

Witnessing a Miracle

WHAT DOES IT mean to experience a miracle? This is a complex question with multiple answers. I think we can agree miracles are beyond our control, our grasp, or our reason. Why is it so difficult to believe in miracles? Where do miracles derive from? Who or what orchestrates miracles? I think it's safe to say miracles are beyond our intellect, surpassing human reason. The only way to accept the possibility of a miracle is through faith. And faith is not meant to replace reason but only the things reason cannot explain.

Many recovering addicts have experienced inexplicable miraculous transformations with inexpressible conclusions or explanation as to the how and why's. In most cases their conclusions were simple, in desperation surrendering to a power greater than themselves for help. The miracle that ensued was beyond their control or reason. So, we can begin by saying "Yes" to God. The God of our creation who has set a table for us to dine with Him some day in life ever after. He alone can answer prayers and heal us in body, mind and spirit. A prayer repeated at A.A. meetings is what Jesus told His disciples and contemporaneously is saying to each of us 2000 years later. "Whenever two or more gather in my name I will be in your midst." St. Francis of Assisi, Italian Catholic thirteenth century monk and saint once stated, "Start by doing what's necessary, then do what's possible and suddenly you are doing the impossible." My own miracle as of 2021 is having over 35 years sobriety. Although life still has its ups and downs (This is our human nature, and it is what we do with it that makes a difference) I will remain sober, please God, as long as I am alive. I believe this with all my heart and will remain close to the Lord on this rocky road I travel. Because of my sobriety, I am able now to see life from the outside in. I can see life from a different perspective and much clearer, more objectively instead of subjectively, and even see the bigger picture of life's journey, I can keep perspective on the meaning of my existence being to love one another, which is all that matters in the end, and I can keep fresh in my mind the brevity of life itself. Moreover, keeping focused on God has expanded and augmented my love for Meg, filling my heart with her spirit that seems to grow as time passes.

In our fifth year of One Bread One Body Scripture study group, another incredible miracle of God's love and power emerged. My friend, cofounder and partner of OBOB Lawrence Chukwu had just spent Christmas in his home in Nigeria. Upon his return, he related how he had noticed a young boy with a massive tumor, the size of a cantaloupe protruding from his face below his eye and next to his nose, while attending a Mass in an open field, because they had no building for a church. After Mass, he asked the priest who the boy with the tumor was, and what was his condition. The priest informed Lawrence that the 14-year-old boy named Ebeke had been afflicted with this tumor for 10 years, and local doctors could not help him. They tried to no avail to cut it away, but made matters even worse, carving out his upper palate in trying to do so. Neither Nigeria nor this small remote village was equipped for this type of operation and the doctors lacked the proper surgical skills. He also related that the boys air ducts were now being blocked and he probably would die within months.

That same evening after Mass, Lawrence was at his parents' home when suddenly there was a knock at the door. It was the young boy's father, Theokatis. He implored Lawrence to try somehow to help his son Ebeke. Lawrence, profoundly moved, but with a feeling of hopelessness, thought how remote the chance to help the boy would be. It would take a minor miracle to get the afflicted boy to the United States from this very remote village in Nigeria. Lawrence was given a picture of the boy and soon thereafter returned to Florida.

At the first OBOB meeting after Lawrence's return to the states, he shared the picture of the young boy, and our small group of 10 to 12 was moved with empathy. We prayed about it and unanimously agreed to take on the mission of urgently getting the boy to the United States for a lifesaving operation. We all agreed that this seemed an impossible challenge, yet we trusted in God's will to provide for us to help this suffering young boy. We believe that God, if it be His will, would provide for us and the direly needed surgery. Within weeks, our Scripture study group collectively raised the money to bring Ebeke, and his father here to the United States. We contacted our local US Congressman to intervene on our behalf with expedited visas. Somehow through the graces of God, we found the means and ways to complete the operations required for Ebeke. It turned out that not one, but two 11-hour surgeries were needed. We prayed to our

Lord to help us find the doctors and surgeons to perform them pro bono since we had not the funds for such an enormously costly operation.

Ebeke, 14, and his father Theokatis, arrived with a tiny suitcase and a brown bag with their belongings. Within days, our OBOB committee began frantically, to arrange for the impending surgeries. Time was against the suffering boy's life. Death was imminent if not for a speedy operation. Time was of the essence. Contacting surgeon after surgeon proved fruitless. The imaging showed hundreds of tiny roots emanating from the massive tumor lodged under his nose and eyes, and the operation was judged extremely difficult.

Figure 2. Ebeke on his way to Miami for his operation.

FINALLY, ONE DAY we received a call from a prominent surgeon who said she would take on the probable multiple surgeries needed, and, moreover, it would be with no charge. The miraculous moment finally came, and Ebeke was flown down to Miami. The two 11-hour surgeries were successfully performed, and the large cantaloupe size tumor was removed, saving Ebeke's life.

Ebeke's physical recovery would take months and required his staying in the states to monitor the healing process. Our members Dominic and Christy Scipione generously volunteered and agreed to house Ebeke and his father with their own children giving up their bedroom for their new friends.

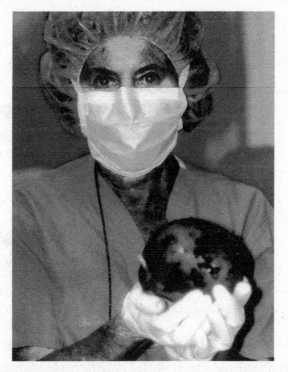

Figure 3. Ebeke's tumor, representing the suffering of the throng of voiceless and faceless sufferers around the world, is also a reminder for all of us that we have a responsibility to reach out and help make a difference.

THIS HEALING SURGERY began with a simple inquiry by Lawrence and the plea by Ebeke's father. As Jesus tells us, "Ask and you shall receive." God provided love and tender care for a young man living on the other side of the world, thanks to the doctors that took on this operation pro bono and to our OBOB that provided financial assistance to get Ebeke and his father to the United States and to OBOB members Dominick and Christy who provided housing not only during his recovery but for the ensuing five years.

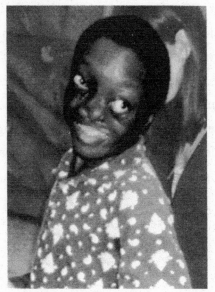

Figure 4. Tumor successfully removed. Thanks be to God.

THE MIRACLE DID not stop after a successful surgery for Ebeke. Soon after his operation, Ebeke attended one of our Bible studies to thank the group in person for all we had done for him. Although his face was badly deformed from 10 years of a growing tumor and now a large cavity on the left side of his face as a result of extracting the tumor, Ebeke was aglow and filled with joy. He was barely able to stop smiling. His father said it was the first time in 10 years that he saw his son smile. He had been teased over the years by his peers because of his radically deformed face. Now he was given hope and acceptance by complete strangers.

During one of our OBOB meetings my wife Meg along with OBOB member Cheryl, both teachers at Annunciation Catholic Academy announced they had arranged for Ebeke to attend the academy through a scholarship. Thus, Ebeke began his two-year stint at the academy and finished as an honor student.

Together in unity, we can all do amazing things in helping in loving others. President John F. Kennedy once said, "One person can make a difference, and everyone should try."

Chapter 18

The Miracle Continues

NOT MUCH LATER, at one of our weekly OBOB scripture meetings Ebeke was present and conveyed to the group the horrific living conditions back in his village. He said his people die prematurely because of a lack of insect repellent, means for proper diagnoses, proper clothing, medications and any means of medical surgery, but the biggest problem was the lack of potable drinking water.

Figure 5. The river in Nigeria from which came the villagers' drinking water, but often bringing serious illness at the same time.

THE MAIN SOURCE of drinking water for this remote village of Umunohu Amakohia, now some 200 years in existence, came from a river that was polluted because animals of all kinds used the same river, resulting in many villagers contracting diseases such as river blindness.

The medical term for river blindness is Onchocerciasis caused by infection from a parasitic worm known as Ochocerca Volvulus. Symptoms include severe itching, bumps under the skin, and blindness. Onchocerciasis is the second-most common cause of blindness due to infection. This parasite worm is contracted by the black fly living near the rivers. The bite of the infected fly implants larvae that grow under the skin; many bites of the black fly are needed before the infection begins. Unfortunately, there is no vaccine or cure for this disease caused by the black fly feasting on polluted rivers. Prevention is avoiding the bite of the flies and use of insect repellent, along with proper clothing. Unfortunately, both are scarce in this remote village. A recent antibiotic called Doxycycline weakens the worms by killing an associated bacterium called Wolbachia, but that medication in the villages is virtually nonexistent. Other medications used to treat river blindness is called Ivermectin that requires an injection every six months to a year. Lastly is surgery to remove the lumps under the skin from the black fly bite.

Ebeke asked our group if there was anything that we might be able to do, and once again, our small group was challenged to respond to his invitation. The need of this remote village in Nigeria was to construct a large commercial well for drinking water. We prayed, meditated and someone stood up and reminded us that, "We have no idea how, or even where, to begin to take on this project, and certainly not the enormous amount of money it would take to construct it." In discussion, the obstacles were laid out on the table one by one. Finally, another person stood and said," I think we should say yes, we will build the well, though we know not how, but if it is to be God's will, He will guide us and show us the way." We exchanged arguments and then finally consented, and our impossible project was placed in motion.

We named the well, 'Mary's Well' as suggested by my

loving wife, Meg. In scripture, Jesus was directed by His Mother Mary in His first miracle at the Wedding Feast in Cana. It was Mother Mary that knew Jesus would change the filled empty jars of water with wine, and it was Jesus and Mary that would help us change polluted potable water to crystal clear water for the villagers. Our project turned out to have many wonderful mini-miracles and soon the whole community of our parish as well as the parish school students aged 5-13 were involved in raising the money needed to build Mary's Well.

Our Annunciation parish school academy invited Ebeke to attend its bake sale which raised over $1000. My six-year-old grandson David raised $375 by asking his friends to bring their extra change and dollars for Mary's Well, instead of birthday gifts to his birthday party. An example of children responding with their love for others less fortunate. On another occasion I received a letter and check in the mail from my eight-year-old granddaughter Rachel. "Dear grandpa, I am going to tell you how I raised $49.50 for Mary's well at my yard sale. I sold lemonade for seven hours! It made me feel wonderful raising money so a village in Africa could have water. I love you, Rachel."

Parents passed the message to their children of sharing with what they have to help those less fortunate, a message that is vital for each generation. It was our 5 to 13-year-old children at Annunciation Catholic Academy that made sacrifices in collecting thousands of dollars for Mary's Well, and for their new friend from Nigeria, Ebeke. The children constructed a model of what Mary's Well would look like and placed it on the ice cream table in the cafeteria. At lunchtime, the children instead of buying ice cream pitched their money into the well. Another example of children raising $1000's of dollars. These are examples again of parents teaching their children of the commands of our Lord. They are examples of children responding to the little voices inside whispering to them," Come follow me", and "Love me and love your neighbors, especially those less fortunate." The young boys and girls knowing they would never see or talk with the children in Nigeria understood in their hearts that there are truly no boundaries to God's love. These are the stories that help awaken the hearts of us adults to meditate on Jesus' teaching that "We must have faith like a child", unencumbered, uncompromised, and unconditional so that we like little David and Rachel, and the kindergarteners will not hesitate but have hearts that respond immediately, "Yes Lord, I will follow." It wasn't more than a few months of the entire community pitching in, a golf outing raising the majority of money along with the remaining donations from parishioner donations and the funds needed to construct the commercial well became a reality. Within a year "Mary's Well" was completed and the villagers had crystal clear water.

My co-founder of One Bread One Body scripture

and outreach, Lawrence Chukwu, myself and wife Meg journeyed to western Nigeria to attend Mary's Well dedication. All the surrounding villages and many different tribes came together to celebrate Mary's Well, a life changing event. We witnessed tears of joy from the villagers. Meg, my wife, was asked to take the first sample drink from the new well after cutting the ribbon and turning on the faucet (spigot). Tears flowed from her eyes as she exclaimed, "It is delicious. Thanks be to God."

We proclaimed to all the myriad of villagers and tribes present that every time they drink from Mary's Well it will not only be fresh clean water, but a conduit of our love from all of us to all of you. We asked for only one favor in return; we asked that they not discriminate against anyone coming to the well, be it race, color or religious differences; and we asked that all be welcomed to partake in the cleansed water of sustainable life. A great lesson and gift we received was realizing that God's love has no boundaries, and that our love should imitate our Lord's.

Upon returning from Nigeria, Meg, Lawrence and I realized that these people had no medical help or medicine to combat diseases that are easily preventable or controlled with medications, which include hypertension, diabetes, malaria, river blindness, and various other infections common in third world countries that are treatable with medication. Premature death is rampant in the villages of

Nigeria. Six months prior to our arriving, Lawrence was there visiting with two of his cousins about the prospects of developing a small business like a fish farm. This would enable their families a way to escape the abject poverty and 90%+ unemployment in the village. They anxiously awaited Lawrence's return in six months. Unfortunately, both in their mid-fifties died before we arrived, due to stroke and heart attack very possibly avoidable had they had the medicine to control the disease. Encouraged by Mary's Well success, our response was an overwhelming 'yes' to build a medical clinic.

Thus, the OBOB group decided to build a community medical clinic adjacent to Mary's Well, of course, with urgency. We did not know how we would raise the kind of money needed for a medical clinic. Again, we called on the children at our parish academy to help, we held another golf outing, and asked many others to contribute to our cause. Thanks be to God! We named the new clinic, St. Luke's Community Clinic. Within three years, our reality of building a medical clinic had come to fruition.

After a number of years, the well built before the clinic required repairs and the same group raised the money for the repairs. Figure 6 on the next page is a flyer from that endeavor.

Rebuild | Refresh | Renew

Providing Fresh Water to The African People

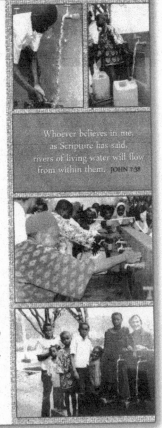

Mary's Well was built in 2003, to supply potable water to Umunoho-Amakohia, Ihitte Uboma, a small village, in Imo state, located about 233 miles south of Abuja, the capital of Nigeria. Many have prospered from its nourishment and sanitary refreshment which has brought joy and gratitude to its benefactors:

> Annunciation Catholic Academy
> One Bread, One Body Scripture & Outreach Group
> St. Mary Magdalen Church

"The gene of thirst has been broken in our generation."

"God, I beg you, bless and keep alive whoever that counted us among those that would have drinking water."

Whoever believes in me, as Scripture has said, rivers of living water will flow from within them. JOHN 7:38

Since it's installation, approximately 245,000 gallons are pumped annually, servicing approximately over 2,000 persons. The deep water well has broken and is in immediate need of repair.

In tandem, nearby, St. Luke's Community Clinic has run low of basic medicine and hospital supplies. They test for bacterial infection, malaria, blood pressure, blood sugar and assist with child delivery.

Funds are urgently needed for this mission of love and well-being. $10,000 would remedy this plight, including services provided by an Engineer to oversee rebuilding of the well. Secondly, the purchase of medical testing kits, supplies and administrative costs would be covered, aiding Reverend Kevin O Madu, Pastor of St. Peter's Catholic Parish, Umunoho-Amakohia, Ihitte Uboma, Nigeria who manages both projects.

Critical refreshment can be restored to this small Nigerian village. We seek monetary assistance and prayers for the continuation of our projects. Thank you!

PART FIVE

Fight or Flight

Chapter 19

A Great Test – Serpent Raises His Head

MY STORY SOUNDS like a fairy tale journey from the darkness of addiction to the incredible joy of the journey out of addiction.

Most everything in my life was as good as anyone could have asked for. A loving relationship with my wife Meg and our eight children (Shawn, Mary, Billy, Stephen, Linleigh, Lesley, Stephen and Erin) along with their spouses (John, Michael, David, Denise, Todd, Errol and Karla) 14 grandchildren and 3 great grandchildren, all healthy, kind, loving people. All with incredible love for each other but also for mankind in general, always reaching out whenever necessary. Financially, we were comfortable, able to pursue most of life's pleasures and able to share our talents and time with those less fortunate. My wife and I were quite active in our churches outreach ministries. All of our children had been baptized as infants in the Roman Catholic Church. All were knowledgeable about their faith and thankfully possessed the heart of our Lord.

The year was 2008—life was good. My sobriety was solid. At age sixty-four, my life had come 180° since my near-death collapse from alcoholism in 1986. I was experiencing a reprieve or a release from the clutches of the Serpent by the power of our loving Savior. I've been asked numerous times how I have been able to stay sober and withstand the temptations to take a drink. Was it your willpower or some miraculous phenomena from some higher power? The only explanation I have been able to give is that I was reasonably sure it was not my willpower alone. Countless times trying to quit over a span of twenty-five plus years had been to no avail. As for some miraculous phenomena occurring, my answer is somewhat nebulous. I can only say of that near death moment, lying on the slab in the ER, I cried out to my Savior, "Jesus, help me Lord. I will quit drinking and I will follow you all the days of my life." From that moment on I've never had an urge to drink again. I can only respond to the question by stating I was a hopeless drunk unable to quit; in desperation I called out to my Savior and have never had an urge since. Soon something would happen though, that would test my faith and my sobriety.

January 17, 2008, was special to me for two reasons. First, because it was the day before my birthday and second, I was to have dinner with two of my sons Billy and Stephen. I called Billy the night before and asked him to call Stephen and get it set for dinner the next evening. He called back and said he called, and Stephen wasn't sure he could afford it, just bought a new house plus having a new 10-month-old daughter Ella. Money was tight he said. Stephen told Billy he'd call him back tomorrow on his lunch break and let him know.

Billy would never receive that call. At 1:30 pm, I received a call, not from my sons, but from my daughter Shawn. "Stephen has been in a terrible car accident, is in the hospital and you must get there immediately."

In my car some 60 minutes—from the hospital, I was in a total state of shock. My only thoughts were How can this be? Just a few days ago Stephen and I were talking at his house, as he picked some beautiful navel oranges from his tree for me, about how he and I would start playing more golf together, and that we should plan another trip to Ireland. Now, driving in a daze, not really knowing the extent of Stephen's injuries or how bad the accident had been, I could only turn to my only hope, our Lord. I prayed *Please don't let it be tragic. Don't let my son be in critical condition. Bless him Lord. Protect him Lord.*

Don't let him be injured badly. It felt like an eternity before I parked the car and rushed into the emergency room.

As soon as I entered, I was greeted by Stephen's wife Karla. Hysterical, and in a stunned state, she fell into my arms as I listened to her speak the worst words of my life: "Stephen is gone."

My heart sank. *Please no. Please no.* Karla inconsolable walked me into the room where Stephen was. We entered and my hopes vanished. There Stephen lay motionless. My son gone. I still couldn't make myself believe this. There was not a scratch on him.

Days after, we would be told the impact was so severe his ribs exploded internally, piercing every organ, and killing him instantly. Three young high school boys skipping school, driving 75 mph in a 25-mph zone, radio blaring, had run the stop sign and T boned Stephen's car.

Now the task for Karla and me was to wait for the rest of the family to arrive, none knowing Stephen's fate. One by one, they all arrived and were taken in to see their lifeless son and brother. His 6'3" body was unblemished—almost like he was asleep, and this wasn't happening. He would come to life again it seemed. Finally, the unbelievable reality set in. Our wonderful son, great friend to his siblings, incredible father to his two daughters, devoted husband, achiever, ready to continue his education with his doctorate degree, lover of life, follower of our Savior, intimate close friend of mine, superb athlete, beacon of love to all who crossed his path, had passed from this life into the next.

A peace began to envelop me. I immediately felt a sense of comfort as if Stephen were trying to tell me, "It's ok, I'm in the arms of our Lord now, in the hands of our Creator, our Master, our Savior," the one he followed every day of his life. Amidst my grief was an assurance that yes, Stephen followed in the footsteps of his Shepherd and Lord, Jesus, and was now sharing in the Peace, Love and Hope of Jesus' message—the promise that whosoever believes in me and follows me will be with me for eternity. In the Gospel of John 14:1-3 in the New Testament it says that Jesus spoke these words to Peter and His other disciples, "Do not let your hearts be troubled. You have faith in God. Have faith also in me. In my Father's house there are many dwelling places. If there were not, I would have told you. I am going to prepare a place for you. And if I go and prepare a place for you, I will come back and take you to be with me, that you also may be where I am."

In a surreal state of disbelief, I instructed everyone to hold hands and surround Stephen, while I retold what was in my heart. "Our Stephen is gone but he was prepared for this day. He lived joyously in this life as an active Christian, had dreams and hopes of someday spending eternity in heaven with Jesus. But for some reason our Lord has called him home. Stephen is there! As children of God each of us is commanded to love God with all our hearts, all of our minds, and with all of our strength and to love and serve one another as Jesus loves us, unconditionally. Stephen's eyes were always on the lookout for someone in distress. His ears always listening for the cries of "Help." His heart thirsting to share God's love, always knowing God our Savior was with him always. Stephen is gone from us, but we are comforted knowing he lived his life as God commanded us to and is now in the arms of his Master and Savior. Stephen has paved the way for us. Shown us the way. In our horrible grief we will comfort and cling to each other. Stephen's spirit will never leave us. Right now, we are all in shock, our hearts are bursting with sadness. But we will together carry on with Stephen's love and memory and example."

The ensuing days of mourning were still filled with disbelief and emptiness. The wake and funeral service drew hundreds and hundreds of mourners. Stephen was a speech language pathologist who helped stroke victims regain their speech. The head of pathology where Stephen worked attended the wake and asked if she could speak to everyone for a moment. "I knew Stephen well and I know he is in heaven for sure. We spent every day together helping others. Each day and each morning Stephen would gather all the therapists and staff and say a simple prayer. "Lord, help us today to reach out and touch someone with your love and make a difference in someone's life."

Life for everyone was extremely difficult, each of us lifting one another's spirit and encouraging each other to stay strong in our faith. I am sure my decision to remain strong in my faith, to stay sober, resulted from God once again putting people in my life to buoy me and help me from falling into despair.

Days, weeks and months tumbled by after Stephen's passing, and the trial of the 17-year-old boy who had been driving the car that hit Stephen was scheduled and set. The day of the trial our whole family as well as the family of the defendant showed up. After both sides gave their testimonies, the judge was ready to announce his verdict and sentence. We reheard the circumstances of that dreadful day: the young boy, along with two of his schoolmates, skipped school and were joy-riding, speeding through a 25-mph speed zone at 75 mph, radio blaring. Not seeing the stop sign, he ran it and T-boned Stephen. The impact of the crash was so violent Stephen's ribs exploded into hundreds of little knives that penetrated every organ in his body and killed him instantly. The boys, instead of summoning help, fled the scene, only to be picked up later by the police. The information was clear evidence of the boy's negligence. The judge had just excused himself to deliberate when, to everyone's surprise our daughters Shawn and Mary rose and engaged the boy, embracing him and telling him he was forgiven. When he returned, the courtroom became silent. The bailiff asked everyone to stand, as the judge sentenced the boy to six years in prison. As the bailiff handcuffed the boy, and escorted him from the courtroom, his family wept bitterly.

Then something miraculous happened. Stephen's siblings Shawn, Mary and Billy stood up, and one by one crossed the aisle and embraced the convicted boy's family. Immediately, the rest of Stephen's family followed suit. No words were necessary because the gesture was silently saying, "We forgive your boy for killing our son, our brother, my husband, my father."

Family members on both sides were blinded by the flow of tears. Surely the Grace of God permeated each of our hearts. The judge, also weeping, exclaimed, "I have never seen anything like this in all my years."

Faith is the only explanation for this extraordinary behavior. In most cases, human nature would have produced a very different outcome. Instead of compassion and forgiveness there surely would have been vengeance and resentment. It reminds us of our Lord's trial and crucifixion. While the people were shouting, "Crucify him, crucify him," the only words Jesus could muster up were, "Father forgive them for they know not what they do."

The ensuing days, weeks, months and years were difficult, and at times challenged our faith, but through prayer we were able to comfort and buoy each other, and through the grace of God persevere. Stephen's death brought us immense pain and sorrow, but it also brought a new awareness of how fragile we are, and clarity as to the meaning of each of our lives, and what God has called all of us to become. Stephen lived his faith so fervently, reflecting the Gospel message of unconditional love, that his death served as a reminder of how precious it is and how brief. Though his death left us clinging to each other with broken hearts, sadness and despair, there was a hidden joy knowing he had lived his life according to how God hoped he would live it—becoming His Light, Love and Hope to all he encountered, especially the lost and broken.

Staggered by my broken heart, I faced a decision: To remain in a state of mourning and despair, or to pick up my cross, carry Stephen with me in my heart, mind and soul and, like Stephen, fulfill the dream God had for me? It would be so easy to give up and retreat back to my old alcoholic ways. Or I could say, "Help me Lord. Touch me with your healing power and strength. Give me the courage to move on. My wife Meg, day by day, gently and tenderly encouraged me to stay strong and reassured me Stephen had prepared himself for the moment none of us can escape.

That moment we take our last breath in this earthly life, and where we go from here depends on how we lived our life before. If we are knowledgeable of the word of God, we know our ticket into heaven in our final judgment will depend on how we love our Creator and how we unconditionally love all others. Even those who are almost impossible to love. Even those we know have no love for us. Even those—who harm us. For we are called to imitate our Creator, our Savior's unconditional love for all of us. Our Savior hates our sinfulness but is willing to forgive us if we are willing to repent. So too, we must love unconditionally, and be willing to forgive those that harm us. Hate the sin but love the sinner.

At times, I have experienced the miracle of receiving the gift of being able to love, like God commands. The miracle happened, not by any decision or attempt I made to love like God, because I believe in almost every case, we mortals love only by our own standards. We have limits on how we love. It seems we are capable only of loving those who in some way love us, or those that we witness having devoted their lives to loving others. The miracle, through the grace of our Savior, came I'm quite sure as a result of a prayer imploring our Savior to fill my heart with His unconditional love. Anything is possible with God. We must ask. Often times our faith is limited by our disbelief. Mother Theresa of Calcutta was a prime example of loving unconditionally. She was a woman of great action and love, but few words, whereas most of us speak many words but with little action. So, as humans, when we hear of atrocities people have committed, we not only despise and hate the atrocities, but also hate the perpetrator of those atrocities. We are unable to even begin to entertain the idea of forgiveness. This is where our love differs so dramatically from our Savior's love. He loves us unconditionally just the way we are. That simple decision to say yes to God allowed me to continue to reach out to others whenever possible and, thanks be to our Savior, in a sober state.

So, what about you? Is or was there an event in your life that has or is crippling your dreams and hopes. Have you ever been in exile? Self-induced exile as a result of sinfulness or guilt or shame, maybe loneliness, fear, hopelessness or hatred towards others. How did you escape your exile? In the Old Testament, the historical figure, Jeremiah, the Jewish prophet during Israel's 40-year Babylonian exile, presented a message to the Hebrew people of repentance and restoration. *Turn back to God away from your sinfulness and God will restore you.* He instilled in the enslaved Jewish nation that their only hope was to surrender to God. He will deliver you out of bondage. There is no other way. Difficult decision but unfortunately no alternatives. Do not fret. Even Jeremiah had conflicts between his own natural inclinations and God's message. He also struggled at times in his own prophetic journey. So, like Jeremiah we must transform our often weak, corrupt heart, the stubbornness of evil that abides in it, to a strong heart, faithful to our Saviors commands.

Who was your Jeremiah? Maybe your spouse, sibling, parent, grandparent, or perhaps a child or friend, maybe a stranger. Maybe something you experienced or heard. Maybe none of those mentioned. Possibly you were Jeremiah to yourself. How could that be we ask? Through the silencing of our mind, heart and soul open to prayer, crying out to God and most importantly waiting and listening for a response. Part of our being, our purpose, our vocation is to become Jeremiah to those that still live in some form of exile. But first we must free ourselves of the bondage that blocks the love, hope and grace of God in each of our hearts and minds. Will you now say no to your Savior's help, and remain silent and die within yourself, or will you, like I did, say yes Lord, touch me with your healing power. I too want new life and want to know you and follow you.

Chapter 20

Breaking Out of Your Cocoon

So, LET'S SIT back and totally relax, pondering and meditating our sincere commitment to change our lives. We've come to a crossroad in life. We must take a new path. Chart a new route back to sanity. What a task! This will take a radical change, yet again a simple decision in merely say "Yes," rather than say "No," in order to begin your first step. Am I up for it? Am I ready? Do I believe God can change my hopelessness, the fear that engulfs me, the shame and unworthiness that shackles me? Do not despair. Do not doubt. The one who formed you in His creation will reshape you. He will cleanse you of your sinful baggage that keeps you mired in chains. He will heal your heart and then transform you into His love.

You however must choose. Do I want to remain as I am, or am I ready to courageously take the first step to change? You must ask yourself, "What will the treasures of this world bring me in the end?" The answer is clear, nothing. The only thing that will accompany you at the end of your life is the history of the love you shared and the good deeds you performed. So, will you be prepared to present that history to your Savior, the one we each will likely meet, face-to-face, in the end; the one who right now is waiting for us to say, "Yes Lord?" So, take a moment to ponder your own life's journey to this point.

So far, some of you may feel like life has dealt you an unlucky hand. Others may feel just the opposite, that they have been blessed, but know deep down inside that they have selfishly squandered a lot of the blessings of life. For example, has there been refusal in caring about others, such as apathy for the poor, that has blinded your awareness time after time with opportunities to help the less fortunate?

Whatever your lot in life is, or whatever hand you've been dealt, we all have something in common. We were all created by our Savior, and have now been given a reprieve, an opportunity to erase what has been done in the past. In other words, we have a chance to be cleansed and forgiven of our past bad deeds, and to walk joyfully forward in a transformation wrought by faith in our Savior. So, let's look at ourselves if we can from the outside in. Let us look beyond, if we can, the deep hole that we are mired in.

By working the first few steps, Step 1 and Step 2 of A.A., you have educated your mind to understand that your life to this point has become unmanageable with no light at the end of the tunnel. You realize that God and only God can restore you to sanity. Now you must take this mindset and include your heart. That is, you must educate your heart, in order to connect with your mind. Once you take this migration or journey from head to heart and courageously examine your inner self and complete Steps 3, 4 and 5 you will experience a cleansing, a renewal, a discovery, and possibly a flicker of hope and confidence within yourself. A sense of freedom will begin to emerge within you. When this occurs, you must take the figurative migration back to your mind, to strengthen and develop this new link between heart and mind, so that you'll be able to respond to the needs and challenges of the world.

Once you reach this point, where you can clearly see life from the outside in, you will then be ready to embark on a study of Scripture to educate your mind, heart and soul. A new spirit will embody you, and, when the timing is right to reach out to those suffering, a whisper from your Savior within you, will beckon you to become a companion, and a seeker of the brokenness in the world.

You will then, like all those that have taken these journeys and migrations, have to decide whether or not you are ready to reach out to others who are mired in the same hellhole you have escaped from. If you answer yes to the soft voices prompting you to reach out to the world's suffering, then you will have taken a migration from your head to your heart to your feet and, so to speak, "walked the walk."

You will intuitively recognize your true purpose in life. You will have taken the full journey and migrated from your head to your heart, to your feet and now back again. You will have allowed your inner journey from your mind and heart to engage with your outer journey in making a difference in the world. You will have the ability to look beyond your present moment, whether ecstasy or agony, and by continuously working the program increase your readiness to reach out when opportunities present themselves. Without this exercise it will be extremely difficult to move forward. The emotions of fear, hatred, remorse, envy, and hopelessness that permeate us, and weave about within us, will shroud any possibility of imagining a life of sanity once again.

We must at this point cast open the windows of our minds and doors of our hearts so we can peer out and get a glimpse of our Saviors hope. A hope and realization that no matter where we are right now, no matter how lost we are right now, God can transform us, reshape us, and restore us to sanity. When we're mired in addiction it's difficult to put ourselves in that position, to look at life from the outside in. The only thing that seems to dominate our thoughts and mind is the torturous emotion that consumes us, preventing us from looking beyond.

The Spiral (Figure 7) illustrates the plight of the addict.

Figure 7: The Spiral

ADDICTS OFTEN TIMES find themselves stuck in the middle unable to see beyond themselves, mired in the black hole of life. In order to look at life from the outside in, a journey is required of one A.A. step at a time. The goal of the addict is to somehow navigate from the middle to the outside in order to be able to once again see beyond themselves.

They get caught in the torment and anguish at the dark center of the spiral. Their goal is to somehow navigate and travel through the spiral from the center to the outside, so they can see themselves in the world from a totally different prospective, free from their present encumbrances. Maybe that seems impossible in your current state. Many that suffer in the clutches of addiction find themselves trapped. You can imagine being in a room with no doors. No place to run, no place to escape from the torment, the unbearable agony, teetering on the cliffs of despair.

Where you think there is no way, God finds a way. By following the steps outlined and with the assistance of others, great blessings and mini miracles will start to occur during your recovery as you work the steps. Slowly you will be able to look at life from the outside in, to be able to look beyond all your travails so you can see life more clearly. The ultimate goal is not to see life as the world sees but rather through the lens of our Lord and Savior.

Figure 8: The Labyrinth

FIGURE 8 ILLUSTRATES a second concept of the journey. As the Labyrinth illustrates, although your goal is to go from the middle to the outside, there will be many roadblocks and traps that can lead you astray, seeking ultimately to vanquish your quest. Heed this warning! If you try and go it alone you will, in all likelihood, fail. Countless others have attempted to do this, but at some point, most have failed miserably. You will need a guide.

Once you reach the point where you can view life from the outside looking in, a calm and a sense of confidence will present itself to you. A mini miracle will evolve. You will realize that God can transform you, reshape you, and restore you to sanity. Our new understanding and faith, knowing God loves us and is with us, not only gives us joy in the good times but consoles us in the dark moments of life.

However, just believing that God is with us may not be enough to sustain us in the desperate times of our life. I can't repeat this enough. We must learn as well who God is, His characteristics, His actions, so we are able to correctly respond to life's challenges. We must also remember what His focus in life really is, His promises to us if we obey Him and His commandments and commit to follow in His footsteps. Thus, it is important what our Savior Jesus told His disciples and what he tells each of us today: "If you make my word your home, you will indeed become my disciples; you will learn the truth (unconditional love); and the truth will set you free." Jesus is telling us to know Him and to understand what He stands for in life. We must be a student of His gospel and the holy Scriptures.

Again, we must understand one essential need. It is not enough to just study His word and absorb it intellectually, we must cry out to our Savior, as we study His word, and ask Him to help us internalize the Word, so we become an embodiment of the Word.

Not coincidentally, as we mentioned earlier, the 12th step of A.A. parallels this gospel command that we seek out those that still suffer. So, let's review again the first few steps. The first, second, third and fourth step. As we allow ourselves to empty all this baggage we've been carrying around, inside and on our shoulders, we will, after diligently and faithfully working these steps, be filled with our Savior's love and spirit. These steps will also allow us to arrive and approach another important minor miracle—to love our neighbors as we love ourselves.

But we must go one step further; we must love them unconditionally. This means, we must be firm in our resolution to become, as we say in our Roman Catholic faith, reconciled. That is, we must become free of any hatred, bitterness, animosity, or resentment within. While forgiving others, we must also be fearless in our examination of conscience, admitting our own past sins, but also all our sins of omission, when we failed to respond.

It's only when we look deep inside ourselves to acknowledge and unmask our weaknesses, our sinfulness, and our past shameful behavior, that we can then plead to our Savior, our maker, and our higher power, to free us from the hell that imprisons us. Likewise, we must also be ready to again reconcile with our Savior, asking for forgiveness, with a priest, our sponsor, or designated confessor. This will be an ongoing action in your life that will keep you full of peace, tranquility, serenity and serve as a reminder and clear vision as to your main purpose in life. So, the time is now, through prayer, to ask God to strengthen you, and give you courage. Do not second guess yourself. Do not fear. Just do it!

At this stage of your recovery, you have admitted that you have a drinking or drug problem, or perhaps some other form of addiction, and your life has become unmanageable. You've made a decision to turn your will and your life over to the care of your Savior. With that assumption, hopefully you are ready right now to begin action time. Ready for Steps 3, 4 and 5, you have decided to work the steps, along with your sponsor, a Catholic priest or minister in your church, or with whomever else you have chosen. Don't be afraid. Your sponsor has heard them all. If you think your confession is going to shock them, guess again. So, be honest, thorough and fearless in your moral inventory. This is important. To begin your confession there are a few prayers you can say beforehand.

The first prayer is the Lord's prayer:

> *Our Father, who art in heaven, hallow be Thy name. Thy kingdom come, Thy will be done, on earth as it is in heaven. Give us this day, our daily bread and forgive us our trespasses as we forgive those who trespass against us. And lead us not into temptation but deliver us from evil, for Thine is the kingdom, the power and the glory, now and forever, Amen.*

The second prayer is called an act of contrition:

> *Oh my God, I am heartily sorry for having offended you and I detest all my sins because I dread what might happen to me in my sinfulness and I fear the loss of heaven and eternal life with you someday and I also fear the pains of hell. I firmly resolve, my Lord, to confess my sins and with the help of your grace, to make amends in my life. Amen.*

> *Bless me Lord. These are my sins.*

SO NOW, WE enter into confession. In a sense, we unclothe ourselves. We come before our Lord crying out for forgiveness. We enter into confession as sinners, full of sin. After confessing our sins, we leave as sinners but without sin. God has cleansed us, let us go forth and not sin again. Make certain you have thoroughly examined your conscience and have not left any wrongdoing out in your confession. Do not sugarcoat this admission. Be bold and truthful and put all your trust in the Lord. Humility is key here. Yes, an impossible task for most of us, but that is why confession is such a wonderful sacrament or phenomena. It allows us, when we do falter and slip, to come back to our forgiving and loving God's mercy and ask for forgiveness once again.

In my own case, this new beginning allowed me to open myself up for healing. The only caveat was that I had to totally surrender, to totally uncover and expose my faults, sins and transgressions. But, having attempted this, I felt a change, not only by blind faith, but by a sense of calm and peace that seemed to permeate my being.

The God who created us wipes away the dark moments in our lives, erasing all of our regrets, shame and fear, placing us on the path of recovery. We no longer have to carry around on our shoulders all the garbage that has tormented us all these years that have deprived us of true happiness and peace. We begin to experience a feeling of forward movement on our road to recovery.

We are now ready to check and measure our life saving transformation. If the love we feel for God, ourselves, and for our fellow humankind, transcends all of our feelings contrary to God's love and forgiveness, we can rest peacefully.

St. Augustine, the fourth century convert, throughout his early life was mired in sinfulness, but had a massive transformation or metanoia (change of heart), in discovering who God is and how God loves us and what awaits us in eternal life, if we choose to follow Him. He had a saying that millions of people 500 years later have cherished. "My soul is restless until it rests in you Lord."

It is said that the person that we love the least represents the amount that we love God. So, we must be on guard and vigilant, alert and cognizant. If our temperament, anger or hateful thoughts towards others exceeds God's love within us, then we need an immediate renewal of heart and confession along with working Steps 3,4 and 5.

Now having been cleansed of our sinfulness, the baggage we carried around us has been emptied, lifted off our shoulders. At this point our mind, heart and soul should be in a more restful, open-minded, serene place. We should now be able to ponder the great gift of our own individual creation, discover who we are and what God commands of us. We discern, learn and clarify these commandments by continuing to study Scripture and more importantly the life of our Savior. Our Savior Jesus' life is a roadmap, a blueprint, as to how we are to live our lives as well. We must become the embodiment of Jesus' love and peace and offer ourselves to the world. Indian Hindu Mahatma Gandhi once said, "We must become the change we seek in the world." So, by receiving this miraculous healing, we are now ready to search out our creator to know him, learn about him, and understand what he wants of us. In a sense we enter into the mind of our creator.

Before we commence on our in-depth study of who our Savior is, through the reading of the old and New Testament, we must ask God to help us internalize His Word rather than merely intellectualizing it. In this way we will develop what is called an informed conscience. We will intuitively understand and know what to do in most circumstances that arise in our life. Our mission is to follow in His footsteps, so we will not only realize happiness here in this world, but manifest great joy and happiness in the world to come.

PART SIX

New Path in Life

Chapter 21

Get Ready for a New Life You Thought Impossible

MY JOURNEY IS probably a lot like yours—in some way being possessed by the serpent and his addictive, cunning ways, especially his beguiling way of drawing us into the darkness of sin. Although my sobriety has been lifesaving, many of my defects of character still exist. Even though my God given gift of sobriety transcends all temptation and compulsion to drink, there is yet a pervasive presence of evil that periodically weaves about within me, and intermittently threatens to rear its ugly head. It is like weeds among the wheat. Too often we fail to realize the power of addiction and its subtle seductiveness. To recognize the more insidious sides of the evils of addiction requires the courage to examine our innermost selves. We must look deep into our hearts and conscience to discover and uncover our fears and insecurities. I feel as if, like a roaring lion, the serpent of endless forms of addiction still prowls around me, waiting for a chance to devour me. That is, though I walk with Christ within me, I am incredibly only one drink away from being a drunk once again.

I must constantly remind myself of two things. First, of God's gift of sobriety, and second, my root purpose in life to become His light to brighten and pass the message of hope to those who still suffer and live in some form of darkness. I am aware that for an addict to be complacent is to walk on thin ice. What about you? Are you ready to walk into the footsteps of our Savior? Are you ready to begin your journey back to sanity?

In our journey back from Serpent to Savior, it is often the little choices we make in our lives that determine the direction we go. The little "yes or no" decisions. You have a choice to make now. You can choose to do nothing and remain in the clutches of the serpent Satan. But know with all certainty that behind that destructive choice lurks a seductive voice opposed to all good and righteousness. Or you can say, "Yes, I will do something," even if perhaps, like I did, you still feel it is hopeless, yet in blind faith, you take that first step on a new path in your life. Even though this step might seem fearful, hopeless or doubtful, do not be deterred. Know with all certainty that God, your Savior, is right by your side and will not let you down. Jesus once said to his disciples: "Come to me, all you who are weary and burdened, and I will give you rest. Take my yoke upon you and learn from me, for I am gentle and humble in heart, and you will find rest for your souls. For my yoke is easy and my burden light." (Matthew 11:28-30)

Maybe you don't suffer from addiction, but you know someone you think is addicted. Act now like my brother Dave did with me. I was offended by his insinuation that I had a drinking problem, but, in the end, it saved my life. So, ask God for the courage to confront that person. Again, you may be the only one in their life that will have the courage to reach out to them before it's too late. We've all heard the horror stories of those addicted whose lives were cut short either by accident, overdose, suicide, declining health or incarceration due to DUI etc. You can be their Savior's hand. It's up to you. It's one of those little decisions we have to make. Yes or no.

For those mired in addiction, I must reiterate that there is no state of sinfulness or unworthiness you may be feeling that could transcend our Savior's Love for you and His readiness to lead you out of your addiction and back to sanity. You don't have to change first. The only prerequisite is to say, "Yes, Lord, I am heartily sorry for all my past transgressions. I need you and I will say 'Yes' to walk in your footsteps. Touch me Lord with your healing power and strength."

Father Joe Young, friend and Catholic priest, works with addicts in a ghetto located in Limerick, Ireland. He has spent most of his life working with those suffocating from addiction, giving them comfort and direction. He once shared this prayer with me:

In the comfort of your love,

I pour out to you my Savior,
    the memories that haunt me,
    the anxieties that perplex me,
    the sickness that prevails upon me,
    and the frustration of all the pain that
    weaves about within me.

Lord help me to see,
    your peace in my turmoil,
    your compassion in my sorrow,
    your forgiveness in my weakness,
    and your love in my need.

Touch me, O Lord,
   with your healing power and strength.

Our sinfulness and sometimes apathy towards
   the least of our brethren, separates us from
   God, blocking out His light, peace and love.

POPE FRANCIS'S SHORT homily keenly illustrates this point. "Whenever our interior life becomes caught up in its own interests and concerns, there is no longer room for others, no place for the poor. God's voice is no longer heard, the quiet joy of His love is no longer felt and the desire to do good fades. We end up being incapable of feeling compassion, the outcry of the poor, weeping for others pain and feeling a need to help them as though all this were someone else's responsibility and not our own."

It's worth repeating—maybe you know someone suffering from addiction. Act now. Have the courage to confront them. You could be the only one in their life who has the courage to do so. Or maybe we think we are righteous and judge addicts as sinners who we think can easily break their addiction through willpower. Maybe we feel comfortable in life, blameless and self-righteous, and confident we are on the right path. If we find ourselves in these particular positions we should shudder with fear of God's condemnation. In the gospel of Luke 18:9-14, Jesus illustrates the danger of falling into that mindset.

"Two men went up to the temple to pray, one a Pharisee (a Jewish leader in religious matters and Jewish law) and the other a tax collector (tax collectors were despised and loathed by the common people). The Pharisee stood by himself and prayed 'God, I thank you that I am not like other people—robbers, evildoers, adulterers or even like this tax collector. I fast twice a week and give a 10th of all I get.' But the tax collector stood at a distance. He would not even look up to heaven, but beat his breast and said, 'God, have mercy on me, a sinner.' I tell you that this man, rather than the other, went home justified before God for all those who exalt themselves will be humbled, and those who humble themselves will be exalted."

Whichever person you may identify with, all can agree there does in fact exist a major problem and that we need God's help because we are totally unable to eradicate the problem by ourselves. Once we establish this, we are ready to start our journey back to sanity. First, let's erase any doubt that God can for certain restore us. Whichever case we find ourselves in right now, we must be ready to turn over our life and will to the care of God. This is a monumental step in humility. Where do I begin.

For me, this moment came when my life had totally broken down physically, mentally, financially, and almost spiritually. On the verge of losing my mind, totally confused, helpless and desperately hopeless, I stumbled by mistake into an A.A. meeting. Making one of those little "yes or no" decisions we talked about earlier I frightfully said yes to get out of the car and walk into the meeting. I was warmly greeted as I entered and immediately felt welcomed. Once seated I listened to the addicts talk about their experiences and their road to recovery. One woman talked about how her life went, from hopelessness to a life full of joy and peace. As she spoke her smile and the excitement in her voice legitimized her story. I'll never forget my thoughts that day listening to her. She gave me a glimpse of hope, but I was sure at that moment that I was by far in a more severe hopeless condition then she had been.

As I continued to listen to her talk about the miracles that would happen to us if we took the first step, I watched her smile. I remember saying to myself what a miracle it would be in my life if only I could smile once again. A simple smile seemed so distant to me at that moment. The meeting ended and I still felt helpless, but now I had a speck of hope. As I was leaving big Bob, as they called him, stopped me and noticed my desperation. He told me not to worry it will get better. Just keep on coming back. I did and soon was working the first step of the A.A. program.

I admitted I was powerless over alcohol and that my life had become unmanageable. Big Bob (or Dr. Bob) became my sponsor. First, he recommended I attend 30 meetings in 30 days. I replied I needed more. I'm suffering badly. I ended up attending 90 meetings in 30 days. Noon meetings, 5:30 p.m. meetings and 8:00 p.m. meetings. I was desperate and would go to any length to feel peace and sanity again. At that point I didn't realized it, but I was off and running on my way to sobriety and recovery.

Like myself you must agree that you are ready to accept the fact that your life is off track and on a slippery slope to destruction. That you've had enough suffering and/or have caused enough suffering and that God and only God can restore you to safety and sanity. If the answer is yes, Great! Let's move on. Next, we "Let go, let God." We must believe without any reservation, that the creator of all who formed each of us can reshape our lives, that right now at this very moment, we are totally surrendering ourselves and our lives to Him, confidently knowing He will come to our aid. We're letting go and letting God take over. Don't second-guess your decision. Ask yourself this question. "How has my decision-making worked out for me so far?"

For me, this moment came soon after I surrendered myself to God and I am confident it will for you as well. If not, go back to the first step and pray this simple prayer over and over. "Help me Lord. Have mercy on me a sinner. Touch me with your healing power and strength. Guide me back to sanity." Hope grew for me as I studied and began to work the second and third steps in A.A. I gradually came to believe that a power greater than myself could restore me back to sanity. In Step 3, I made a decision to turn my will and my life over to the care of God as I understood Him to be.

Let's stop for a minute and discuss the state we are in. We've failed miserably and now clinging desperately to God to restore us to sanity. Sound easy? What if we have no personal knowledge of this God or any personal relationship with Him, what do we do then? Where do we begin? My answer is to just believe. Move forward in blind faith. Sometimes when things of God are beyond our reasoning, are unexplainable, inexpressible or incomprehensible we just believe. There are no alternatives. Just say "yes" to God. He formed you in His love and He will, if you ask, sustain you in His love. The following is a simple, beautiful prayer for those who are engulfed in fear and despair:

Lord my Savior. I come to you burdened with
worries, fears, doubts and troubles.

Calm and quiet me with peace of mind.

Empty me of the anxiety that disturbs me, and
of the concerns that weary my spirit and
weigh heavy on my heart.

Loosen my grip on the disappointments and
grievances I hold onto so tightly.

Release me from the pain of past hurts, of
present anger and tension of future fears.

Sometimes it is too much for me, Lord.

Too many demands and problems, too much
sadness, suffering and stress.

Renew me spiritually and emotionally. Give me
new strength, hope, and confidence.

Prepare me to meet the constant struggles of
daily life with a deeper faith and trust in
you.

Let your love set me free...
For peace, for joy, for grace, for life, for
others, forever.

AT THIS JUNCTURE on your path to recovery it is vital and quite imperative that you seek out a sponsor. The sponsor will, with total confidentiality, guide you through the 12 Steps. Equally important is to find a sponsor with many years of sobriety, if possible. You are about to embark on possibly the most difficult steps in the program—Steps 4, 5 and 6.

There are certain beliefs in Christianity that are

analogous within each and every one of our different faiths, whether we are Jewish, Muslim, Hindu, or have any other God-fearing beliefs. I would venture to say this is true even with agnostics and atheists. One belief, whatever God you believe in, I think we all can concur with is God is love and He desires all His creation to become that love in the world.

The Catholic Church teaches that through the sacrament of confession or reconciliation Jesus forgives us after we confess our sins to a priest, and by the power of the Holy Spirit the priest absolves us of those sins, cleansing us and giving us new life. So, whether you are a Catholic or some other Christian denomination or maybe Jewish or Muslim, Hindu, Buddhist, agnostic or atheist the key component for you right now is trust and belief. With this belief and attitude, you will now be able to move on to sit and ponder your life, both the good times and the bad.

Make sure, however that you work Steps 4, 5 and 6 closely with your sponsor or the person to whom you intend to confess your sins. This will consist of writing down all the sinful things you have done throughout your life. This may be painful but it must be done. It is absolutely imperative that you make an honest and fearless thorough inventory, a list of all your past transgressions and sins. This takes immense courage, but we want to uncover and expose all the bad that we've done in life, metaphorically speaking, up to this point. To develop in a sense an x-ray of our life.

This is important. This is the first step in becoming a new person, shedding the old skin of the person struggling hopelessly and adrift. We will become renewed knowing God has forgiven us and loves us unconditionally. To believe anything less or to think our sinfulness is greater than God's love for us, is an utter insult to God. It is only through a repentant heart and mind that we can begin to decide to let go of everything that torments us or blocks us from the light and peace of Christ.

We must surrender to our Savior in order to let God in and to cleanse us, to restore us, to empty all the baggage, and to heal our blindness so we can see again as the Lord sees and feel His love for us, ultimately so we can love ourselves once again. And then and not until then will we be ready for the next step, and that is to confess our sins.

Chapter 22

In His Footsteps

UNFORTUNATELY, WHAT WE read about earlier in my story is probably a lot like your story, where the serpent got in the way and sucked you into his addictive ways, drawing you away from the path of our Savior. Let's continue as we embark now on our new journey fresh with the confidence that we are in the guiding hands of our Savior. But what does "following Jesus" mean to me, if I do not even know Jesus? Well, whatever your faith, or lack thereof, is at this point, the Commandments Jesus gave to His disciples were then, and are today, just as relevant. He said, "You can take all of the Commandments and reduce them to two. The first, "Jesus said, is to love the Lord your God with all your heart, with all your soul, with all your mind, and with all your strength."

The second resembles it: "You must love your neighbor as yourself." He went on to tell his disciples they should love one another unconditionally as He loves them. That is a tall order since Jesus gave His life for all of us.

The next step is to learn more about who our Savior is, how He thinks, what He would do in any particular situation. By diligently taking these steps, and learning who Jesus is, and what he commands of us, we are given something unique and most precious in the world which we inhabit—an informed conscience. In most cases it allows us to instinctively know not what the world thinks or wants, but more importantly, to intuitively discern what God our Savior thinks and wants.

So again, although you can find God's love within the walls of A.A., I recommend studying the Holy Scriptures, which includes the Torah or Old Testament as well as the New Testament. Again, it tells the story of how God created the world, how He created man and woman and the journey and stories of God's people over the past 4000 years or so. The New Testament picks up where the Old Testament leaves off, and tells the story of Jesus,

God's only begotten Son, how He was sent down from heaven and what He commanded His disciples to do. These commands as I mentioned before are transcendent in time and apply today to each of us who follow in His footsteps. It is said that the New Testament is concealed in the Old Testament and the Old Testament is revealed in the New Testament.

The gospel of John might be a good place to begin your study. Be mindful, however, to go about this study with some form of guidance. Either seek out a bible study guidebook or obtain a commentary on whatever you are about to study. You might want to attend a Catholic Mass or service at a church and visit the bookstore at the church to obtain a commentary. Also, as I mentioned earlier, seek out a A.A. sponsor, who has a lot of sobriety. He or she can guide you along the way. The best way to make sure you do not misinterpret what you read in scripture might be to seek help from someone at the church you attend or call the church office and inquire as to where you might find help. If that is not feasible you can call any Catholic Church and ask them about the RCIA program.

This is an ancient study dating back to the fourth century church. It delves into all of the other religions of the world. This enables us to get a glimpse of each faith, helping us to understand the tenets of that faith a little clearer, allowing us to dialogue with others of that faith more open-mindedly. Most importantly it is God's knowledge of what and how each of us are called to live our lives. This understanding of God's commands gives us an educated mind in unison with our Savior's and allows us to make right decisions going forward on life's journey. I suggest and highly recommend seeking this study out. It will open your eyes, heart and mind as to what your purpose in life is.

In summary, I would personally recommend unequivocally the RCIA study, the study of the Holy Bible, and the study of the A.A. Big Book. Before each study session, pray to our Savior for His guidance as you read and study the Word to enable you to internalize it at the same time. This will help you unlock and open the doors to true peace and joy, given only through the power of God, not found in the temporal treasures of the mortal world.

As a result of this delving into Scripture, a thirst and hunger will develop in you, as it most certainly did in me, to become more Christ like. In a sense you will begin to shed all of the fears that have imprisoned you and don a new cloak, become a new self, one that loves and forgives yourself and others unconditionally. In time, as God heals your heart, this fruit of learning and getting to know who God is, and how God thinks, will be your transformation into His love. Eventually, you will not so much talk the talk as you will walk the walk.

So, where do we go to begin to understand who God

is? In order to imitate him, we must know who he is, and how he would respond to the events of the world that await us. Since God is love and knowing and believing He created us in His love, is with us now, and will sustain us in His love on our earthly journey, we are confident when our moment comes to cease to exist in this world, He will bring us home in His eternal love.

Of course, there may be other ways to know and experience God and His love. One may be to say a simple prayer, asking God to transform you into His love, to empty your heart of any hatred, resentment, regret, fear, or a host of other negative feelings. "Jesus, my Lord and Savior, if it be your will, transform me; empty my heart and fill it with your divine unconditional love." This little prayer takes great unwavering faith but know without any reservation that God will and can do anything you ask in His name, if it be His will. Jesus once remarked "When you call in distress, I hear you."

In the New Testament Bible, Jesus tells the story of Bartimaeus and how his faith cured him. They came to Jericho. And as he was leaving Jericho with his disciples and a sizable crowd, Bartimaeus, a blind man, sat by the roadside begging. On hearing that it was Jesus of Nazareth, he began to cry out and say, "Jesus, son of David, have pity on me." And many rebuked him, telling him to be silent. But he kept calling out all the more, "Son of David, have pity on me." Jesus stopped and said, "Call him." So, they called the blind man saying to him, "Take courage; get up, he is calling you." At that, he threw aside his cloak, sprang up, and came to Jesus. Jesus said to him in reply. "What do you want me to do for you?" The blind man said to him, "Master, I want to see." Jesus told him, "Go your way; your faith has saved you." Immediately he received his sight and followed him on His Way.

Bartimaeus had absolute unwavering faith. He knew that if he could just somehow reach Jesus, Jesus could and would give him sight. A cloak for a blind man was like a safety shield, to guard and comfort and in a sense protect him from all harm.

But when they called Bartimaeus to come to Jesus,, he sprang up, and threw aside his cloak, throwing away his only security and putting all of his trust—100 percent—in Jesus. We must have the same unwavering faith as Bartimaeus. That said, in order to realize our Savior's effectiveness in transforming ourselves, there must be a total absence of all doubt. Like Bartimaeus we must cast away all disbelief.

Another way we may experience God, is simply observing our friends as they give of themselves for the benefit of others. In the thirteenth century, a rich Italian merchant's son, Francis of Assisi as he was called, was selling his wealthy fathers' silks in the town square when a beautiful young girl named Clare came up to buy them. Just when she was about to exchange her money for the expensive silks, a poor hungry mendicant came up to her and began to beg. Moved, she suddenly gave the money to the beggar instead of buying the expensive beautiful silks. Francis, inspired and in awe, was so moved by this unselfish act that soon after he completely turned his life over to Jesus. He spent the rest of his life tending to the poorest of the poor. The Franciscan Friars and priests, who follow the order of Francis of Assisi, number in the thousands today. They tend to the poor in every nation worldwide. Francis' motto and instruction to his friars was "Preach the Gospel of our Lord at all times. If necessary, use words."

This universal prayer, written about Francis of Assisi, is repeated by millions worldwide:

Lord make me an instrument of your peace,

Where there is hatred- let me sow your love,

Where there is injury- pardon.

Where there is despair- hope.

Where there is sadness- joy.

O' Devine master, grant that I may not so much seek

To be consoled- as to console

To be understood- as to understand

To be loved as to love.

For it is in giving that we receive,

It is in pardoning - that we are pardoned,

It is in dying to oneself that we are born to eternal life.

ONE PERSON CAN make a difference. Little decisions change lives and in many cases the course of history. In your journey back, it will often be the little choices you make that will determine the direction you go. You have a choice to make now. You can choose to do nothing and remain in the clutches of the serpent Satan or you can act now by saying I will take the first step. It's up to you. It will be easy to think about shaking your addictions, make excuses, dismiss the idea and move on with your life.

In any case I must first preface your first step back by saying there is no state of sinfulness or unworthiness you may be feeling that could transcend our Savior's love for you and His joy to lead you back out of your addiction. He is ready to take you back right now and you don't have to change first. The only prerequisite is to say "Yes Lord, I am heartily sorry for all my past transgressions. I need you and I will say 'Yes' to walk in your footsteps. Touch me, Lord, with your healing power and strength."

As a result of this transformation, we have been given new life and are sent out into the world as His love, light and hope to feed those broken, who live in some form of darkness and to give others new life. This love that now abides within our minds and hearts is a gift from God and it is not meant to be kept within us. It is a gift that we are called to share.

> "A bell is not a bell until we ring it, a song is not a song until we sing it, love wasn't put into our hearts to stay, love isn't love until we give it away."
>
> —Oscar Hammerstein II

Having through the power of our Saviors' spirit been changed into believers in Him, we are now ready to become followers as well. Jesus tells His followers, "They will recognize you as my disciples by your love."

Do not be alarmed, dismayed or doubt this impending change in your life. It probably won't come overnight. It will come in God's time, but it will for sure, if you follow his commands, come. Again, in God's time.

This transformation for me during my recovery came after I worked the 12 Steps, gone to hundreds of A.A. meetings, studied Scripture from cover to cover, read the A.A. Big Book, read the A.A. 24-hour meditation book and attended Mass weekly. I also became involved in bible studies along with praying incessantly. But don't be intimidated by my journey. I grew stronger day by day, one day at a time, week by week, month by month, year by year. I started from that black hole in the Spiral totally lost, totally hopeless, nearly totally helpless and nearly spiritually and financially bankrupt. So, I know from my own experience traveling from that black hole in the Spiral where I could only see myself and my seemingly unsolvable, insurmountable predicaments, that it is possible to travel that Spiral and Labyrinth to the point where I can see from the outside looking in and to start to regain my sanity.

Again, do not be fooled into thinking you can make this journey without your sponsor. If you do, you will be disappointed. The most important thing is to believe at this point in your journey, in your recovery, that God will with all certainty transform you, heal you and use you as His love and peace in the world. Do not doubt. Take up your faith, rejoice and be glad, for right now the God who formed you in the palm of His hand knows where you are in life, knows the torment that's weaving about within you, but is smiling because you have repented and are hungering and thirsting for His love, miracles and promises to happen in your life. So, as we begin to look at ourselves from the outside in and get a glimpse of where we are in life we can once again begin to dream of the possibilities that can take place if we maintain the courage, and continue on our journey taking these miraculous steps.

My journey in life, I guess like most of us, has been mixed with many blessings along with many disappointments and struggles. But the greatest blessing for all of us now is that we are able to look beyond our grief to recognize and discover the irreplaceable gift and blessing of each of our creations. Regardless of how many joys or disappointments we have had in our lives up to this point, we must now look at our existence with a keen sense of gratitude. We must somehow overlook the bad things that have occurred in our life and gratefully understand we've been forgiven. We must focus on the good things that we have done in life or the good things that lie ahead for us as a result of our soon to be recovery and dream about the possibilities of the future. When we are mired in our addiction and we find ourselves in the middle of that Spiral, we become consumed with ourselves, unable to see the surroundings and have fallen into a dangerous situation. We are only able to look within ourselves. When that happens, we die. That lonely, tormented place can ultimately lead to depression, sickness, despair and even suicide.

But now after taking the steps to regain our sanity through our recovery we are able to look beyond ourselves and our own travails and somehow become new people, disciples. It allows us to look beyond our darkness, and, as a result of this transformation, allows us to get a glimpse of the needs of others. We eventually attach ourselves to those needs and become generous to those needs of others. Mother Theresa once exclaimed, "If you want to find yourself, lose yourself in the service of others."

We become a living spirit. We will become dual citizens, citizens of this world and future citizens of heaven. Hopefully having made this decision to follow and become our Lord's love and hope in this life, we understand that this will surely force us to sacrifice ourselves and to enter situations of discomfort, loneliness and fear as a result of this change. We will be catapulted into the threshold of the next key to our joy today and road to salvation in the next world. The key to action in becoming the Word of our Savior.

There is an old Hebrew aspiration that goes like this:

To see as God sees-To know as God knows-

To feel, O feel as God feels-To be as God is.

As a result of our renewal, we have clothed ourselves with the cloak of Christ. We know what we have been called to become. We must respond to that call. In our daily prayers we cried out to God for mercy and forgiveness. We begged him to heal and fill our hearts hungry for His love. We thirsted and hungered for total transformation of our mind-body and soul. And now we pray to be sent out to become His light in a world filled with divisiveness and darkness, to give love to those filled with hatred, and to give hope to those gone astray and lost. Irish priest from Dublin, Bishop Dermot O'Manohey in one of his homilies once exclaimed, "Wherever you cannot find love, put love. And then you will find love."

We hear our Savior calling to us softly in the recesses of our heart: "Do not be afraid. Come follow me. Do not fear. I am with you now until the end of time." This is where and when we must act. Dependence and trust in our Savior are like a wellspring of eternal life that will never fade away or dry up. Trust in man or this world is a temporary quench. It feels good now but will suddenly dry up and disappear, leaving us withered and dead. Again, we must choose. Trust in our Savior and live or trust in the flesh and die.

As a result of developing an informed conscience we intuitively are capable of discerning what is pleasing to our Savior or pleasing to the world and how we respond to events or decisions facing us. Do we follow our

Savior or follow the world? Perhaps we should challenge ourselves by asking ourselves a seemingly basic but profound question, I once heard by Franciscan Priest Fr. Patrick Quinn. Are we Americans first who happened to be Christian, Jewish, Hindu Muslim or are we Christians, Jewish, Hindu's, Muslims first who happened to be Americans? If my answer, is I'm a Christian who happens to be American then I again become confronted with the questions, "Who is my neighbor?" "Am I my brother's keeper?" "Are there borders to God's love?"

When we ponder theses questions and are truthful with ourselves, in a way we unlock the key to our primary mission in life and realize although we differ in so many ways throughout the world, we are really connected as children of God. Our vocation in life's journey is to love God and love one another unconditionally. In the gospel of Luke, we recall Jesus was asked "And who is my neighbor?"

As individuals, as a family, as a nation when we ask ourselves these difficult questions, "Who is my neighbor?", Am I my brother's keeper?" Or "Are there borders to God's love?"

How do we respond?

Do we, as followers of our Savior, become the Good Samaritans as Jesus suggests or do we follow what the world's logic is telling us and pass on by those who are in need?

We must and can say, "Yes Lord" and follow His beckoning or choose to remain silent. The choice is ours. The stakes are high. Will we follow our Savior the Lord or follow the world? We cannot follow both. We must choose between them.

Chapter 23

All Roads Lead to Rome

AS IN ANCIENT Rome, where all roads ultimately lead back to the city of Seven Hills, the many roads each of us have trod in our lives, finally lead back to one place also. Some roads we choose lead us on journeys of success in life, others lead us down the path of failure and destruction. Some may lead us on the path of godliness sharing our talents and treasures with others, while others lead us down the path of self-centeredness and

selfishness, either knowingly or unknowingly. Some of
our roads are mired in sin and addiction while others are
paths of prayer and righteousness. No matter which road
in life we find ourselves on, there is one thing for certain;
all roads will eventually one day lead all of us to this same
place. That place is the day, the hour, and the moment
when our earthly journey ends, when we take our last
breath, and cease to exist on this earthly plane.

No matter who we are, no matter how our life has been
to this point, whether rich or poor, healthy or sick, sad or
happy, powerfully influential or ordinary citizens, none
can escape this encounter and moment. That moment
for each of us will be the most significant moment in
our existence because it is at that moment, when death's
door opens, when we each will experience the incredible
face-to-face, one on one encounter with our Creator.
No matter what our religious beliefs may have been in
life, Buddhist, Hindu, Muslim, atheist, agnostic, Jewish
or Christian, none can escape their encounter with our
maker.

I, as a Roman Catholic Christian, realize at that
moment we will encounter our Lord and Savior Jesus
Christ. He will then judge how we lived our earthly life
and what roads we chose to take. During our earthly
time, we were constantly asked to choose between good
and evil. During our addictive years we often times made
the wrong choices. Hopefully after you have decided to

change, studying who God is, you will then have another
clear choice when temptation once again arises. Be
certain of one thing, the temptations of the Serpent will
always be lurking and waiting for you to slip up.

The important thing to understand, to ponder and
to realize right now, is that for each of us at that moment
of encounter with our Savior it may be too late less we
have a repentant heart, to change anything. In Matthew
25 (Verses 31-46) Jesus talks about the end time:

> *But when I, the Messiah, shall come in my glory,
> and all the angels with me, then I shall sit upon
> my throne of glory. And all the nations shall
> be gathered before me. And I will separate my
> people as a shepherd separates the sheep from the
> goats, and place the sheep at my right hand and
> the goats at my left.*

> *Then I, the King, shall say to those at my right,
> come, blessed of my father, into the Kingdom
> prepared for you from the founding of the world.
> For I was hungry and you fed me; I was thirsty
> and you gave me water; I was a stranger and
> you invited me into your homes; naked and you
> clothed me; sick and in prison, and you visited
> me.*

Then these righteous ones will reply, "Sir, when did we ever see you hungry and feed you? Or thirsty and give you anything to drink? Or a stranger and help you? Or naked and clothe you? When did we ever see you sick or in prison, and visit you?"

And I, the King, will tell them, "When you did it to these the least of my brothers you were doing it to me!"

Then I will turn to those on my left and say, "For I was hungry, and you wouldn't feed me; thirsty, and you wouldn't give me anything to drink; a stranger and you refused me hospitality; naked, and you wouldn't clothed me; sick, and in prison, and you didn't visit me."

Then they will reply, "Lord, when did we ever see you hungry or thirsty or a stranger or naked or sick or in prison, and not help you?"

And I will answer, "When you refused to help the least of these my brothers, you were refusing help to me."

NOTE THAT THE people he referred to as goats, also called Jesus, "Lord," but during their lifetimes they chose to look beyond helping those in need. We will probably be asked one question, "How did you love during your earthly life?"

The exciting thing is that right now we all have time to change and turn our lives around. The simple fact is that we are still alive and have the chance and opportunity to ponder that great moment of encounter and have the opportunity right now to decide to change our lives. Or if we already think we have changed, and are on the right track in life, perhaps we should take another look at ourselves.

Earlier we read about how Jesus spoke about this in His parable about the Pharisee and the tax collector. Maybe we should get a second opinion. This little pondering of our life's end could well be our greatest gift and secret to restoring our sanity. It not only warns us of what each of us will face in the end, but pondering that magnificent moment gives us immense clarity as to what we should do presently and how we should live our lives from this point on.

Again, let us remind ourselves that the moment of judgment is a moment none of us can escape and we know not when our time will come. Jesus said we will not know the time nor the hour. He will come like a thief in the night. So, we must be vigilant. We must stay awake.

We must understand that we are living our judgment right now.

"Seek ye first the kingdom of God then all else will be given unto you." We must constantly pray for God to continue to show us the Way. We give thanks for forgiveness, for the healing and for our transformation and pray to be sent into the world as His light and His love. So, after much meditation and study we hopefully will have made this decision to follow our Savior, to become our Lord's love and hope in the world. We also must understand that this will surely force us to sacrifice ourselves and to enter situations of discomfort, loneliness, and fear. Becoming a light to the world does not call us to detach ourselves from the sinful darkness of the world, but rather calls us radically to immerse ourselves into the darkness of the world.

Jesus associated with sinners to touch them with His love and give them a chance for redemption. If we just love and associate with those we already love and turn our heads away from those that have drifted off the path of salvation, we, to a degree, add to their demise. By remaining silent we become accomplices. What good did we do? Even the sinners love each other.

Let us not forget the 12th Step of A.A. Having had a spiritual awakening as a result of these steps, we try to carry this message to alcoholics, and to practice these principles in all our affairs. The completion of the 12

Steps, will be of vast importance to you. It may seem rather obscure right now, but after completing the program, you'll understand this step clearly.

At the same time, once you have a solid sobriety and you are thinking more clearly and your life has become manageable once again, you must remember the gift and the miracle that you have received and become a seeker of those who are still suffering. Although we are not called to sit around the circle and sing "Kumbaya," it is vastly important during your recovery and even after to fellowship with like-minded people, to strengthen and encourage one another.

We are also called to individually turn to our Savior to be healed and forgiven, but then turn and strengthen our brothers and sisters that are still out there, so they too may receive and experience saving grace, hope and salvation. As true followers of our Savior, this calling asks us to bring light into the trenches of sinfulness, despair, hopelessness, brokenness and darkness. There is a great paradox where we cry out to become the light but are then cast into the darkness. But make no mistake, by giving of ourselves for the sake of others; we are soon satiated with the love, peace and joy of God our Savior and Creator.

I will caution you though that until you have experienced recovery or transformation and gone through all the 12 Steps of A.A., you probably are not strong enough and may risk succumbing once again to temptation and find yourself in the same spot of those you seek to help.

Another simple prayer that we can whisper throughout the day is "In the dark of night, Lord, keep me always in your sight so to others I might become your light."

Not only will this study of Scripture allow us to enter into the mind of our Creator, because it is the Word of God, it also will give us tremendous clarity as to how we should live our lives and what the true meanings of them really are. Jesus once told his disciples, "If you make my Word your home, you will indeed become my disciples. You will learn the truth (unconditional love) and the truth will set you free."

I might add that a lot of this unconditional love also lies in the book of AA and within the walls of AA meetings. So, this truth that you will learn through the study will unlock the door to true joy and peace given only through the power of God and certainly not found in the temporal treasures of the mortal world. In our darkest moments, it is a peace the world cannot give.

As a result of this delving into Scripture, a thirst and a hunger will develop to become more Christ-like and shed the fears that imprison you. A hunger and thirst to don a new cloak, and become a new self—one who loves unconditionally, and has the capacity to forgive unconditionally. By this surrendering to God our Savior, we become a seeker of those still imprisoned, those still suffering, those still chained to addiction and to those still living in darkness from guilt, shame and sinfulness. By crying out to God, we can be transformed into His new person, to become His light in a world full of darkness. To become His presence for those clinging to the sinful lures and treasures of the serpent and the world. Joy will replace the turmoil and sadness within you. Peace will stamp out the fear that permeates your mind. Faith will raise you from the abyss of doubt and the light of our Savior will dispel the darkness that has paralyzed the possibilities of new life.

But to do this He sent us commandments. One commandment is to love God with all your heart, with all your strength, with all your soul, and with all your mind. The second is much like the first. To love each other as we love ourselves and to love and serve others unconditionally. He went on to say to his disciples and he says the same to each of us today, 2000 years later. If you believe in me and follow the will of my Father, you will experience eternal life with me. If so, we will become that spirit, that love, become like our Savior himself in this world. That means we will share what we have and give to those in need. Our heart will become exactly like his. Burning from within to love everyone, especially the unlovable, the ones that even hate us, including our enemies. We will be called to hate the sin but love the sinner. By following our Savior, we will become His hands and reach out to those beaten down with despair and hopelessness. We will become His feet and walk in the places where we normally would not go. We will become His eyes to seek out those who are lost in life. We will become His ears to hear the cries of anguish and injustice in the world. And we will become His heart to feed the great famine of love in the world. Where we find those starving for love, we will pray to instill love in hopes the emptiness we encounter will be filled. To understand that we possess the God that we seek in the world, we realize that we possess a spirit within us, an insatiable love for all, destined to forgive others, and by using us as a conduit of His love, transform all those we encounter, and reach out to those whose lives are lost and broken.

So, we need to stay connected to our Lord, to remain tethered, lest we find ourselves adrift in the dangerous waters of the world. Pray for His Holy Spirit to remind us to stay close with our eyes fixed upon Him. If we lag behind, our minds occupied with too much of the world around us, we risk losing sight of our Savior. And if we lag behind too far, we become prey to the evils waiting in the wings, ready to pounce, waiting for us to slip, forget what our true life's purpose is and our true destination – Heaven and Eternity with God. So, we must stay awake always, remain vigilant and focused on keeping up with our relationship with our Shepherd, lest we err and veer off His path to the path of sinfulness and death.

What a gift. What a challenge. This is our chance. This is our opportunity. Let us now make an appointment with our Lord.

Chapter 24

Make an Appointment with the Lord

SUPPOSE WE WANTED to make a doctor's appointment. What do we do? We pick a day, a place, and a time. So, let's do the same thing and make an appointment with our Savior. The place should be a spot away from the noise of the worlds' cacophony of voices and beehive of daily activities vying for your time. This will be a time to intimately speak directly with our Savior and Lord.

We have already established that our addiction has

caused our life to be unmanageable and we need God to rectify this by bringing us back into a state of sanity. Let us not forget relying on the world and oneself limits us because we almost always overestimate the power of ourselves and underestimate the power of God. Leo Tolstoy once said, "The more we live by our intellect the less we all understand the meaning of life."

We pretty much concur that up to this point our lives and our decisions have pretty much failed miserably. So, as we await this upcoming appointment, where we will let go of ourselves and let God take over, it is important to allow ourselves to consciously see ourselves as we are now and have a clear vision of whom we hope to become, through the grace of God, in the days, weeks, months and years ahead. We now must seek the faith to let go of ourselves and let God take over. Let go, let God.

Belief and trust, its constant companion, will be the key components. It may seem a blind preposterous belief, but we must simply trust and just believe. Sometimes the unexplainable, the inexpressible, the incomprehensible cannot be understood by our limited intellect. When we embrace and depend on God, it allows us to imagine. So, in most cases where doubt and skepticism creep into our thinking, the only alternative is to trust and just believe. It's safe to say the vast greatness of God's power is limited by people's lack of belief.

So, let's go, if possible, to a quiet place where we can

try to focus our thoughts on God's greatness and the possibilities of Him touching our lives. According to Socrates, the great Greek philosopher, "Wonder is the beginning of Wisdom." Try to get a feel for the immensity of our world, the unfathomable explanation of creation, and finally the miracle of your own creation. Take a few moments just to meditate on that phenomena. You are seeking to convene with the Creator of all that is seen and unseen. First humbly ask God to help you quiet yourself. Thank him for helping you to develop a new attitude of gratitude.

Focus on yourself. No matter what your lot in life or what juncture in your life's journey you're at right now, thanking your Savior for the fact that God thought of you and created you is the most significant event in your life. Why so significant? It matters because you, in your uniqueness, were created by God to live and enjoy this beautiful world, and according to God's Word, may live eternally with him in the world to come.

Once you ponder this monumental moment in your life, you have uncovered the first key to peace, joy and hope in this life and the world to come. Do not be afraid to ask God to transform you, heal you, and catapult you out of your agonizing and painful lifestyle. But again, I caution you, if you think for a moment that your sins of the past or present are too great, or possibly too egregious for God to forgive, forget it. God loved us so much he shed his blood for us even amidst our sinfulness. So, to think your sins are greater than God's love and forgiveness for us is an insult to our Savior. Cast away any doubt of your worthiness. God is ready to reshape you into a new person just as you are.

JESUS SPOKE THIS parable of the prodigal son and his brother. "There was a man who had two sons. The younger of them said to his father, 'Father, give me the share of the property that will belong to me. So he divided his property between them. A few days later the younger son gathered all he had and travelled to a distant country, and there he squandered his property in dissolute living. When he had spent everything, a severe famine took place throughout that country, and he began to be in need. So he went and hired himself out to one of the citizens of that country, who sent him to his fields to feed the pigs. He would gladly have filled himself with the pods that the pigs were eating; and no one gave him anything. But when he came to himself he said, 'How many of my father's hired hands have bread enough and to spare, but here I am dying of hunger! I will get up and go to my father, and I will say to him, "Father, I have sinned against Heaven and before you; I am no longer worthy to be called your son; treat me like one of your hired hands."So he set off and went to his father. But while he was still far off, his father saw him and was filled with compassion; he ran and put his arms around him and kissed him. Then the son said to him, 'Father, I have sinned against Heaven and before you; I am no longer worthy to be called your son.' But the father said to his slaves, 'Quickly, bring out a robe—the best one—and put it on him; put a ring on his finger and sandals on his feet. And get the fatted calf and kill it, and let us eat and celebrate; for this son of mine was dead and is alive again; he was lost and now is found!' And they began to celebrate. "Now his elder son was in the field; and when he came and approached the house, he heard music and dancing. He called one of the slaves and asked what was going on. He replied, 'Your brother has come, and your father has killed the fatted calf, because he has got him back safe and sound.' Then he became angry and refused to go in. His father came out and began to plead with him. But he answered his father, 'Listen! For all these years I have been working like a slave for you, and I have never disobeyed your command; yet you have never given me even a young goat so that I might celebrate with my friends. But when this son of yours came back, who has devoured your property with prostitutes; you killed the fatted calf for him! Then the father said to him, 'Son, you are always with me, and all that is mine is yours. But we had to celebrate and rejoice, because this brother of yours was dead and has come to life; he was lost and has been found.'"

The words of Socrates are relevant here: "The unexamined life is not worth living." You can now begin that examination by looking at yourself from the outside in. Reflect on your own beginning and journey in life. Try to get a clearer view of who and where you were, where you are today, and where you should tread henceforth. At this point try to focus on just the blessings you have experienced in your life's journey and give thanks.

Right now, as you are reading this, there is God's ray of light, penetrating through the darkness, through the fear and despair that's weaving about within you, a light ready to lead you back to sanity. Give thanks for that, and the opportunity for your recovery back to joy, solace and peace within, as well as the discovery of who you are, the true meaning of your life and what you are called to become on this earthly journey.

Our journey in one sense has to come to an end. The life we once lived according to our will alone has come to rest because one must die to oneself in order to rise anew in Christ. We live again with Christ who lives within us. We must decide to follow him. We must choose yes or no. Yes, I will follow and act, and do what the Spirit prompts me to do. Listen to the soft voice within your hearts beckoning you to say "Yes." Or we may choose to say, "No," and remain in the old self, remaining silent, and dismissing the calls from within.

The stakes are high. We must be reminded; it is not enough perhaps to just believe in our Savior Jesus and do nothing else. We must believe and live the gospel, and in doing so, become an extension of His Spirit and Love. When we do this, and depend on God, it allows us to imagine what possibilities lie ahead of us.

I myself must confess it has been mostly during the low points of my life that I drew closer to and more dependent to God. In the agonies and ecstasies of my life, I have discovered that it is in—becoming the same being, the same spirit and the same Love of my Creator, that each of us finds contentment and complete solace.

We have all been wayward and adrift with the sins and lures of the world, have experienced life's mountaintops and valleys, but in the end we most glow with His Love, for His son Jesus warns us that, out of all these experiences in life, we will be judged only on how we loved.

We live this life as dual citizens. Citizens of this world and future citizens of heaven. When they come into conflict, we have the words of Jesus to guide us: "Render therefore unto Caesar the things which be Caesar's", and unto God the things which be God's." Jesus's words show

His awareness of potential conflicts and that it is not necessary to be superhuman. We were created to love God with all our heart, with all our mind, all our strength and all our being and to serve him by loving and serving mankind as His Son Jesus our Lord and Savior loves us. This high standard should realistically be interpreted as "Do your best," which is plenty high enough.

You can now look beyond where you are at this moment and fast-forward to that glorious moment when our earthly journey comes to an end. This may sound morbid or frightful, but if we are truthful and have the courage to work toward it, it will change our life.

So now the time has come to sit with your Savior, friend, and God. Let not your heart be troubled. Do not fear. Start by sitting in a comfortable position either in a chair, on the ground or possibly kneeling. Relax and simply ask God to be with you. Now try to relax all your muscles starting with your forehead muscles down to your cheeks, your mouth, your neck, your shoulders, your arms, your hands, your fingertips, your chest, your stomach, your hips, your legs, your feet. Now you should be totally relaxed and free of any tension.

Now simply and softly ask the Lord to be with you and fill you with His peace and serenity. A beautiful prayer read at each A.A. meeting goes like this:

God grant me the serenity to accept the things

I cannot change,

The courage to change the things I can,

And the wisdom to know the difference.

NOW SPEND JUST a few moments thanking the Lord for being with you. The Lord already knows your heart, he already knows your thoughts, but take a few moments in silence, and know that your Savior is here with you.

A few simple relaxing exercises I use may help. Take several deep breaths and slowly inhale the words, "Be with me, Lord." As you slowly breathe out, release all negative thoughts, and exhale all anxiety. Again, slowly inhale the words "Be with me Lord." Exhale any fear. Inhale the words again, "Be with me Lord." Exhale all doubt. Inhale the words, "Have mercy on me Lord." Again exhale any doubt.. Inhale three times the words, "Come Jesus come." Exhale each time any other negative thoughts that arise. Again spend a few moments in silence.

Now pray from your heart just a few words what your heart is speaking to you. Tell the Lord what you want Him to do for you. Then quiet yourself. Silence your mind, and soul to hear the whisper of your Savior.

"Ephphatha"—Be open. Open the ears to hear. Listen...listen...listen.

(Ephphatha) is an Aramaic (or Syriac) word found only once in the New Testament, Mark 7:34.."Be opened"

CLOSE YOUR APPOINTMENT with a simple prayer in your own words. The Lord doesn't care how eloquent the prayer is. He knows your heart, so speak from your heart. My personal prayer goes like this:

Almighty father, I thank you for meeting with me. I deserve nothing but I humbly come before you and ask you for your forgiveness. You know, Lord, my heart. You know my mind and each of my thoughts. You know the torment that weaves about within me. Touch me, Lord, with your healing power and free me from the bondage that enslaves me. Empty my heart and soul of all that is evil and fill them with your unconditional love so I may become a disciple of yours, Lord. Help me to love unconditionally like you. Strengthen me as I take the first step in my journey back to sanity. When I falter, Lord, be there for me, pick me up, and gently place me back on the path of renewal and salvation. Make me a conduit of your love and an instrument of your peace that I may take your spirit and love into the world and touch all those

I encounter. Be with me, Lord and Savior, guide me and shield me from the sinfulness of the world all the days of my life. Amen

So, as we close the last page of this book, we begin a new chapter in the story of our lives. Though we have walked in the darkness of addiction, the serpent no longer controls us. Consciously aware of our creation and that God controls us, we live out our lives with a clear sense of purpose, a definitive path and direction, a confident knowledge of God's love for us and hope for not only the joy, peace and happiness of this earthly journey, but an unmistakable assurance that when our time here ends, we will pass into the arms of an awaiting Savior softly greeting us by name, **"Welcome home faithful servant."**

THE JOURNEY

Let us keep our eyes affixed on the vision of our heavenly home. That is our ultimate goal. We have come to a crossroads in life. We need to take another road home. The road to eternal life. The time we each spend here on earth is not our final destination. Time is merely the ship that takes us there. We are all sharing in this same moment in time, aboard the same ship that is carrying us home to the eternal shore. That is, we are all on the same journey.

J» JOY AND JUBILANCE of realizing our own creation. What God dreamed we would become. The realization that Almighty God chose each of us to be part of Creation. That he dreamt each of us would grow to love Him with all our hearts, minds, strength and soul and someday decide to become that love and share it with the world.

O» OBEDIENCE. To obey the commands of our Lord and Savior. Love and serve God with all our hearts, unconditionally, by loving and serving one another unconditionally.

U» UNIVERSALITY OF GOD'S LOVE. To love all mankind and to join in solidarity with all God-fearing people worldwide. Our Love becomes one with our fellow man, just as in Christ Jesus our Savior.

R» REPENTANCE. WE must continually ask for God's mercy and forgiveness. Fully knowing He can and will if sought. Have mercy on me Lord, a sinner.

N» NEW LIFE. Knowing who we are. Our mission. Our purpose. Children of God. Loving and serving God opposed to serving the world.

E» ETERNAL LIFE. We seek first the vision of eternal life with our Lord and Savior. This vision transcends all things and most importantly gives us enormous clarity as to how and why we should conduct our lives.

Y » THE GREAT AMEN. "Yes Lord, here I am. Yes, I will follow in your footsteps, now and until the end of time." Indeed, we are throughout life confronted with choices. We hear God's soft voice within our hearts beckoning us to "Come follow me." But other voices intervene to confuse us, often even a cacophony of views which conflicts with God's. The Wiley Serpent Satan is always trying to get us to say "No" to God's voice. We can say "No," remain silent and move on, or say "Yes Lord, here I am. Yes, I will follow you," though it will require sacrifices of time, pleasure and personal treasure.

I HOPE AFTER reading this book you will decide to say "Yes Lord" believing He will be with you now and in your final hour with outstretched arms welcoming you home.

PATRICK THE SHEPHERD BOY

Liam Lawton is a multi-platinum, Irish, singer-songwriter and Roman Catholic priest. He wrote a song about St. Patrick called "Patrick the Shepherd Boy." Patrick, when he was 16 was taken by a group of Irish raiders and brought to Ireland to be sold as a slave. He spent the next 6 years working as a sheep herder until he managed to escape. During his time in captivity, Patrick had turned to his faith to help him through this difficult time. These lyrics reflect the feelings, prayers and reliance Patrick had with his Savior and Christ.

Christ be with me, Christ about me. Christ be with me as I go.

Christ before me, Christ surround me, Christ within, above, below.

Christ encircle now my heart, Christ encircle every part.

Christ be with me, Christ about me, Christ be near and never part.

Christ to guide me on my journey. Christ to shield me from the night.

Christ to lead me on each journey, Christ my Hope, my Light, my Life.

Christ to save me from all sin. Christ to call me deep within.

Christ to lead me on my journey, Christ my heart so ever filled.

PATRICK LATER BECAME a Catholic Bishop, eventually returned to Ireland, and converted the pagan country to Christianity.

EPILOGUE

Thank you for reading my story and my journey from Serpent to Savior. My hope is that you will come to the conclusion that you as well can experience the same miraculous recovery, discovery and transformation, and decide without hesitation to take the first step.

"I once was lost, but now am found.

Was blind but now I see."

—Amazing Grace by John Newton & E.O. Excell

CLOSING PRAYER

Yes Lord, I thank you for your love,
and I thank you for your love that abides
within me,
and I say yes to discipleship,
to become your light in the world full of
darkness,
to bring hope to the hopeless,
to reach out with your Love to those lost and
broken, especially to the poor.

Lord, reshape me and count me amongst those
who will live with you for eternity. Amen

IRISH BLESSING

May the road rise up to meet you.

May the wind be always at your back,

May the sun shine warmly on your face,

May the rains fall softly upon your fields,

And until we meet again,

May God hold you in the palm of His hand.